The Church Case Scenario

How to Survive and Thrive in Church

Bruce & Stan
Bickel   Jantz

PROMISE PRESS
An Imprint of Barbour Publishing

The
Church
Case
Scenario

ISBN 1-58660-577-1

Published by Promise Press, an imprint of Barbour Publishing, Inc., P.O. Box 719, Uhrichsville, Ohio 44683, www.promisepress.com

Member of the
Evangelical Christian
Publishers Association

Printed in the United States of America.

5 4 3 2 1

Contents

Church School

Church Youth Groups

Church Picnics, Potlucks, and Retreats

Introduction

Here's something you may not know: More people are involved in church than in any other organization or activity. More than sports, more than music, even more than professional wrestling. Church is a common experience shared by tens of millions of people every single week.

Yet statistics tell us that more than half of all people who go to church while growing up end up leaving the church once they become adults. If you're a "glass is half empty" kind of person, then you would say that the church loses fifty percent of its members. If you view life from a "glass is half full" perspective, then you would say that fifty percent of all people survive the church.

We are "glass is half full" kind of guys who grew up in the church and survived. We've seen the good, the bad, and the ugly of the church-case scenario. And we can honestly say that the good far outweighs the less attractive elements. That's why we can recommend church to anyone adventurous enough to give it a shot. We aren't experts—in fact, we're far from it—but we know a good thing when we see it. And even though we've found a lot to laugh at in the church, we've found even more to love.

That's what makes *The Church-Case Scenario* so unique. We aren't afraid to find humor in the quirky and unusual scenarios that happen only in church. But we also know there's a serious benefit to being involved in church (after all, the church is God's idea). Drawing upon the nostalgic memories and positive experiences of anyone who has ever darkened the door of a church—whether it was in Sunday school, a high school youth group, the Sunday morning service or the church choir—we make a case for appreciating rather than avoiding church. In fact, not only is it possible for you to *survive*, but we're confident that you can also *thrive* in church.

We had only two rules to guide us in writing this book, and we'd like to pass them on to you:

Rule #1: Don't take yourself too seriously.

One of the biggest problems in church today is that people are far too serious, mainly because they focus on themselves way too much. We develop concrete ideas about the way things should be in church, and when someone else doesn't agree with our particular viewpoint, we get hurt, defensive, and upset. That's not what church is all about, and it can make for some unnecessary conflicts. Most of the time these conflicts aren't over big doctrinal issues, but rather nitpicky things that should be a matter of preference, not belief. That's why we've taken the liberty of poking fun at some of the church preferences we all hold so dear. By seeing how silly some of these church-case scenarios really are, maybe we can get down to the truly serious matters.

Rule #2: Take God seriously.

Now here's where we should be serious, but that's not always the case. Have you ever noticed how casually people treat God? Rather than honoring and praising Him as the all-powerful and all-loving God of creation, we see God as some kind of buddy who doesn't mind when we goof up. We are so concerned when other people offend us, and yet we never think about how we might be offending God. We shouldn't live in fear of God, but we should take Him seriously. That's why we have concluded each section in *The Church-Case Scenario* with a little reminder of who God is and what He expects of us.

So have fun as you read this book. For some of you it may be a stroll down memory lane, and for others *The Church-Case Scenario* may be the push you need to get involved again. Whatever your perspective, we hope it all adds up to an encouraging look at the world's greatest institution (and we mean that in a good way).

Bruce & Stan

CHAPTER 1

How to Determine What You Should Wear to Church

You cannot underestimate the importance of proper apparel at church. Actually, God doesn't care what you wear, but all of the church people do (or least it seems that way). If your attire deviates from the acceptable church standard, you will feel awkward and out of place, and the church people may consider you to be (a) a rebellious Christian; (b) a defiant heathen; or (c) a naïve and vulnerable target for intensified salvation efforts.

Consequently, you should plan to attend the church of your choice dressed according to its acceptable dress code. Make every effort to be guided by this overriding fashion principle: blend in.

Unfortunately, all churches do not share the same dress code. Every church has it own version. Garment guidelines for each church are determined by a variety of diverse factors, ranging from the median age of the congregation to the effectiveness of the church's heating and air-conditioning system. When you attempt to anticipate the appropriate apparel for any particular church, keep the following principles in mind:

① **Regional Customs**

Church attendees in the Northeast tend to be more formal than those in the West. If you attend a church in Boston or New Hampshire, you should plan on dressing like Ward or June Cleaver. In Southern California, you might be overdressed if you wear a T-shirt and shorts (depending upon the church's proximity to the beach).

② **Denominational Differences**

Each denomination has a heritage that impacts the congregation's view of acceptable church clothing. If the denomination can trace its roots back to the Pilgrims or the Puritans, you are limited to formal or traditional styles, but you can choose whatever colors you wish (so long as they are white or very dark, but no single item of clothing can have a combination of both). Other denominations will allow you a bit more fashion flexibility. Regardless of their theological differences, almost every church has a certain segment of its population dressed in polyester.

③ **Worship Style**

There is a correlation between a church's musical preferences and its dress code. If the music is old, slow, and comes from a hymnal, you will want to make sure that your clothing selections are from the *Modern Maturity* catalog. On the other hand, if the church platform is cluttered with drum sets and guitar amps, you won't find neckties on the men or hats on the women (except for Old Navy baseball caps).

Despite the reliability of the aforementioned principles, you can't know a church's dress code for certain until you actually attend the church. This presents a problem on your first visit to the church because you don't want to walk through the entrance of the sanctuary wearing clothes that are inappropriate. If that happens, you run the risk that a disgruntled usher will take sadistic pleasure in exposing your fashion faux pas to the entire congregation by parading you down the center aisle and seating you in the front row. To avoid the dangers of being inappropriately dressed at your first visit, here are two fail-safe strategies:

Strategy #1: Dress yourself in layers. Start with the most casual of your outfits. On top of those casual clothes, put on a layer of something that is a bit more sporty. The next layer should be an ensemble that is more traditional. Your final layer should be formal. Immediately upon entering the church lobby, ask an usher for the location of the rest room. Make sure that you have observed the clothing of the people in the lobby before entering the rest room. In the privacy of one of the stalls, disrobe as necessary to the layer that matches the prevailing style worn by the church members.

Although extremely effective, Strategy #1 has several distinct disadvantages: (a) You may have to leave several layers of clothing in the bathroom stall; (b) layering promotes wrinkles, so you'll end up looking stylish but rumpled; and (c) upon entering the church, you will look very puffy. You can avoid these drawbacks by pursuing Strategy #2.

Wally is wearing the perfect church attire. If he wants to impress his church friends with his athletic ability, he can wear the letterman's sweater. If he wants to appear humble, he can easily remove the sweater.

Strategy #2: Before leaving from home, fill the backseat of your car with an assortment of clothing. Include a variety of outfits, covering a sartorial spectrum from casual to formal. With your backseat adequately stocked with apparel alternatives, drive to the church dressed only in your underwear. Park close enough to the church so you can observe the clothing of those on the premises. (Binoculars and a notepad might be helpful.) Be careful not to park so close to the church that members who live nearby will walk past your car. (Using binoculars while wearing only underwear will probably violate your community's antistalking ordinance.) After you have determined the acceptable dress code for the church, discreetly slither into the backseat from the front seat. (Do not exit the front door and enter through the rear door.) Dress yourself in a suitable outfit and then drive into the church parking lot.

If all of this "clothes consciousness" is too much for you, then look for a "home church" in your area. A "home church" is simply a congregation of a few families that meets in a house instead of a church building. We suspect that the "home church" tradition was started by someone who wanted to attend church in pajamas.

CHAPTER 2

How to Decipher a Church Bulletin

To most people a bulletin is a special report or a news flash, usually on the radio or television, as in: "We interrupt this program for a special news bulletin." To someone who spends a lot of time in church on Sunday mornings, a bulletin is a folded piece of paper telling you everything you need to know about the "service." Think of it as a guide or program (only *bulletin* somehow sounds more spiritual).

If you are new to church—or the bulletin still confuses you after all these years—here is the church-case scenario for deciphering this piece of paper:

① **As soon as you walk into the church sanctuary or meeting room, you will be handed a bulletin by a friendly person known as an usher.**
Do not take the bulletin casually. You need to grasp it firmly so none of the extra "inserts" spill onto the floor, creating an embarrassing scene for you and the usher.

② **Do not look at your bulletin until you are seated.**
It will be too much of a distraction as you attempt to

step over several people on your way to the only
available seat in the middle of the row.

③ **Once you are safely seated, open your bulletin.**
First, remove the inserts and set them aside (more
about these later). Familiarize yourself with the overall flow of the service so there will be no surprises.
Check the name of the church and the date. This
will confirm that you are at the right church on the
correct date.

④ **If you are a first-time visitor, scan the bulletin for
important information.**
See if your bulletin includes a tear-off form visitors
will be asked to fill out. If so, start filling it out now
to save time later. More importantly, check to see if
visitors will be asked to stand up and give a brief tes-
timony. If this is the case, take out a three-by-five
card and begin making an outline of your life story.

⑤ **After you have familiarized yourself with the order
of service, check the rest of the bulletin.**
Some churches print a summary of the financial
budget and giving to date. It's important to check
this area because a severe budget shortfall may be a
clue that the pastor will be making a lengthy appeal

for funds during the service, resulting in a longer-than-usual "offering."

⑥ **Turn the bulletin over and look at the section marked *Church Staff.***

Here is where the full- and part-time church pastors and staff are usually listed, along with phone extensions and E-mail addresses. See if anyone new has joined the church staff since your last visit. It's important to know this, especially if you are a life insurance salesman.

⑦ **If you are satisfied that you have become familiar with the entire bulletin, you can now look at the inserts.**

Church bulletin inserts generally fall into three categories:

- Announcements of special conferences and retreats
- Sign-up sheets for special projects and mission trips
- The sermon "outline," which usually bears little resemblance to the sermon you will actually hear, because the pastor had to submit his outline by Friday, and he didn't begin working on his sermon until Saturday night.

⑧ **Congratulations! Now you are ready to "enjoy the show."**

This is only if you attend a contemporary community church with a drama team and a jazz worship band. If you attend a more traditional church, you are ready to "participate in the worship service."

As you can see, deciphering a church bulletin is no small matter. It may require up to fifteen extra minutes of time, so if you want to go through all the steps listed above before the service actually starts, you should plan to get to church early. That's not so bad. Not only will you be more relaxed in church, but you'll get a great parking place.

CHAPTER 3

How to Handle the Offering Plate

Every church service has a moment of supreme self-consciousness. No, we aren't talking about when the preacher gives the altar call. We are referring to that moment when you are handed the offering plate. Unless you are adequately prepared with the proper techniques and strategies, your palms will be so sweaty that you are likely to drop the plate on the floor, causing a big ruckus. Fret not. If you comply with the following suggestions, you can avoid offering awkwardness.

① **It's in the Bag**

There are basically two types of offering receptacles: the offering bag and the offering plate. If your church uses the bag, then you've got nothing to worry about. Your "bagging" techniques will depend upon what you plan to deposit into the bag:

Currency. Most people want to display the fact that they are putting *currency* in the bag. God isn't impressed with the amount of your contribution, but church gossips consider it to be important. Be careful to hold the currency in your hand in such a manner that the denomination is not revealed. If you carelessly show a large denomination, you'll appear to be bragging. If people can see that you are only putting in a single one-dollar bill, then it would be better to put in nothing (as discussed below).

Coins. You must be particularly careful if you are putting coins in the bag. There is a telltale sound that coins make when they hit the bottom of the bag (as they jingle with the coins that were previously placed in the bag by the other tightwads in the church). Hold the coins tightly in your fist. Insert your fist deep into the bag. Extract your hand with a flourish so that any jingling sound will be attributed to the jostling of previously deposited coins as you remove your hand from the bag. (After all, no one will suspect that you gave only coins if you carry out this procedure with dramatic flair.)

Nothing. You can pull this off, but it might require a little practice at home. You have to make a fist with your hand that looks like you are holding something. Insert your hand past the rim of the bag. (Do not put your hand all of the way into the bag or else people might suspect that you are using the "coin" technique.) Once your hand is below the rim of the bag, open your fist and spread your fingers apart. Simultaneously extract your hand from the bag. If exercised with perfection, this technique will give the illusion that you placed currency into the offering bag with such humility that you avoided revealing the currency during the insertion move.

Never make the classic blunder of taking your hand out of the offering bag with your fist closed. (This is often a rookie mistake for those engaged in the "nothing" technique.) If you are seen pulling a closed fist from the offering bag, people will automatically assume that you are making a withdrawal from the offering bag. There is a substantial likelihood that you might be roughed up by a few ushers in the parking lot after the service.

② Getting It Over the Plate

Dealing with an offering plate will require much more delicacy on your part. There is no fabric to conceal your movements. You will have to rely entirely on sleight of hand.

Currency. Whatever bill you place into the plate is going to lie there, exposed for everyone else in your pew to see. If you are going to put in a large denomination (which in most churches is a five-dollar bill or higher), then a single fold of the bill will give the appearance that you attempted to be discreet; yet you will receive admiring looks from your fellow pew sitters as they notice your generous contribution (and believe us, they will notice). If you are only putting in a one-dollar bill, then you must be sure to fold down the corners if you want to avoid major embarrassment at your stinginess. Also, crease the bill so it is folded tightly; you don't want George's face popping out to expose itself as the plate moves down the row.

Coins. Don't let that piece of decorative felt glued to the bottom of the offering plate fool you. Coins still make a sound when they are dropped in the plate. You must place your coins in gently. Try to place them on top of currency in the plate to buffer the noise.

Nothing. There is no fail-safe technique for faking a contribution when the church uses an offering plate instead of an offering bag. Your only hope is to avoid the maneuver entirely. As soon as the offering begins, you must bow your head and close your eyes to appear as if you are praying. Mouthing a few words to yourself may help with the ruse. If the people around you have any spiritual sensitivity at all, they will pass the plate around you rather than interrupt your moment of meditation.

③ **Sealed for Your Protection**
Some churches make the mistake of providing

"offering envelopes" in each row. If a church member puts his or her name on the envelope, then the church can keep a record of cash contributions of each member for income tax deduction purposes.

If offering envelopes are available to you, then you can ignore the bagging and plate techniques discussed above. Simply pull out your wallet from your pocket or purse and pretend that you are putting something in the envelope. Be sure to remember to write a fictitious name on the envelope to make this entire procedure appear genuine. Simply drop the envelope in the offering bag as it passes, or place the envelope face down in the offering plate (so as not to reveal the fictitious name).

If your church doesn't provide offering envelopes, it may be worthwhile to buy a supply of your own from a neighborhood Christian bookstore.

CHAPTER 4

How to Know When to Stand Up and When to Sit Down

There is one sure way to tell the difference between a church-going veteran and a rookie: The veteran knows the correct times to stand up and sit down during a Sunday morning church service, while the neophyte is clueless. In the interest of promoting harmony and unity among all church attendees, here is a church-case scenario for the proper times to stand and sit.

Sit down: When you first enter the room where the church service is held, it is important to sit down as soon as possible. Standing in the aisles to catch up on the latest church gossip creates a hazard for the ushers.

Stand up: Sometime during the first part of the service, you will be asked to shake the hands of the people sitting near you. This "meet and greet" time can only be done in the standing position.

Remain standing: Do not sit down immediately after

the meet and greet. The song leader will most likely lead the congregation in one or more hymns or choruses. This is an excellent time to discreetly wipe off the hand sweat of the people you have just met.

You may be seated: At the conclusion of the singing, the song leader or moderator will say, "You may be seated," and then, to reinforce his words, make a downward hand motion. If the song leader fails to do this, be sure to look around to see what the veterans are doing. If the signs aren't definite, it is acceptable church service etiquette to slowly go halfway into a fully seated position, and then nonchalantly return to a standing position if you notice that nobody else is sitting. However, once you have fully committed to sit down, it is best just to remain seated, even if the rest of the congregants are still standing. Suddenly springing back to a standing position will only call attention to yourself and your red face.

Remain seated: With the exception of the "Hallelujah Chorus," you are not required to stand during any other musical features, including, but not limited to: the organ prelude, the offertory, the choral anthem, and any other special music. Resist the temptation to give the special soloist a standing ovation, even if you think her performance rivals the Anne Murray concert you attended at the Veterans Auditorium.

Stand up: When the congregation is asked to recite the Lord's Prayer, the Apostles' Creed, the Westminster Confession, or any "responsive reading," you will be asked to stand up. As you rise to your feet, reach for the church bulletin, where the words for these readings are usually printed. If there aren't any printed words (which means you are expected to know the material from memory), you can mask your ignorance by simply repeating the word "watermelon" over and over again as you stare straight ahead with a pious look on your face.

A current trend in churches is to give people technical "Stand up/Sit down" training. Here a group of young people is being instructed on the most efficient method for standing up in church.

Sit down: It is usually not necessary to stand during the pastoral prayer. However, be prepared for a change in protocol, such as when the pastor extends the "invitation" at the end of his sermon.

Stand up: More typically, the pastor will ask everyone to stand for the "benediction," which signals the end of the service. It is not appropriate to let out a big sigh or turn to the person next to you and say, "Wow, I thought that would never end!"

Space does not allow us to review the proper "stand up/sit down" protocol for Catholic and Orthodox churches. If necessary, consult your local church procedures manual, and always wear your seat belt to and from church.

CHAPTER 5

How to Stay Awake During a Boring Sermon

Most preachers deliver a sermon that is worth staying awake for. But every once in a while, even the best pulpit pounder has an off day. To preserve the dignity of your pastor, and to avoid your own embarrassment, you need to develop techniques for staying awake on those rare Sundays when the sermon is a dud.

① Doodling

This is a traditional technique. It was this very method that prompted the invention of the church bulletin. People needed a place to make their doodle drawings (someplace other than on the inside cover of their Bibles). If the preacher in a church is consistently boring, then the church might even provide little pencils in the pew rack. Church officials will insist that those stubby pencils are for visitors to fill out a registration card, but now you know the real reason.

② Mental Games

You aren't likely to fall asleep if you keep your mind stimulated. We suggest trying to remember the names of all fifty states. For people who are more spiritual, attempt to mentally recite the names of all sixty-six books of the Bible.

3 **List Making**

This is a combination of both the "doodling" and the "mental games" techniques. In addition to keeping you alert, this strategy has the extra benefit of making you look like you are taking notes on the pastor's sermon. Other people in the church will consider you to be deeply spiritual if you can extract noteworthy insights from a sermon that they consider to be boring. (Caution: Make sure that you write your list discreetly. They won't think you are very spiritual if they can look over your shoulder and see the words *Minnesota, Mississippi,* and *Missouri* on your paper.)

4 **Visual Hypotheticals**

There may be times when you might be stranded in church without paper or a writing implement. (Sometimes those little pew pencils are worn down, and it isn't from being overused by visitors filling out registration cards.) If you can't doodle and are too groggy to make lists or play mental games, try to stay awake by stimulating your ocular muscles and your imagination at the same time. As you stare at the preacher, squint your eyes and try to imagine him in a Hawaiian shirt. How about looking at the organist and picturing her in a ballerina's tutu? Can you squint hard enough to make any three choir members look like Larry, Moe, and Curley? (Caution: Don't employ this technique for an extended duration. When your eyelids are already heavy, prolonged squinting may actually facilitate dozing off.)

⑤ Isometric Exercises

You can't do jumping jacks to stay awake, but try employing a few muscle exercises that can be discreetly performed without major body movements—for example, clenching and stretching your toes. You can even clench and stretch your fingers without being noticed if you fold your arms and put your right hand under your left armpit and vice versa. Another very effective technique is to lock the fingers of your right hand with the fingers of your left hand, and then pull your arms in the opposite directions. Creating equal but opposing muscle tension will keep you awake because it accelerates the blood flow to your brain. (Caution: Don't let your fingers slip. Otherwise, you'll end up simultaneously slugging the people sitting on either side of you.)

⑥ Discreet Sleeping

Sometimes you might be tired and drowsy when you walk into the sanctuary. When this happens, you already know that you are probably going to fall asleep during the sermon (even if it is a really great one). In such cases, you can't fight the urge to sleep, but you can plan ahead. Sit in the back row of the church. You need to be able to lean your head against the wall to avoid that whiplash, jerking motion when your head falls forward as you doze off. (Caution: If there is a possibility that you will snore, then prop one of those pew pencils between your jaw and your sternum to keep your chin from dropping open as you slumber.)

Frank thinks he has the perfect solution for staying awake during a boring sermon. On Sunday mornings he slips out of the service before the pastor begins preaching and goes to the beach.

CHAPTER 6

How to Interpret Church Terminology

Before we get too far into this book of church-case scenarios, we need to take a look at some of the terminology that is unique to the church. These are words and phrases that may mean one thing in everyday usage and something entirely different when used in the context of the church. Just so there isn't any confusion, here are some of those words—many of which you will find in this book—along with their dual definitions. This is not a comprehensive list, by any means. Think of this list as a study guide so you will know how to interpret church terminology on your own.

Accountability Group

People think it means – A group of CPAs getting together for lunch.

What it means in church – A group of men getting together at 5:30 A.M. to study the Bible or a Christian book with the title *Men in Crisis*.

Amazing Grace

People think it means – An older woman who has lived far beyond her life expectancy.

What it means in church – The most popular song in the church hymnal.

Anointing

People think it means – To ceremonially install someone into an official position, such as "He was anointed as the king of Jordan."

What it means in church – A special blessing of the Holy Spirit, usually reserved for members of charismatic churches.

Backslider

People think it means – Some sort of lower lumbar massage device.

What it means in church – Someone going in the opposite direction than God wants them to go.

Become a Member

People think it means – Joining some sort of exclusive and expensive club.

What it means in church – Joining some sort of exclusive and expensive church.

Believer

People think it means – Someone who believes in everything Oprah says.

What it means in church – Someone who believes in everything the Bible says.

Bible Study

People think it means – Boring meetings where people learn about an ancient book.

What it means in church – Exciting meetings where people learn about God's Word (at least they *should* be exciting).

Body

People think it means – The main thing, as someone's body of work.

What it means in church – The main thing, as in the body of believers, or the church.

Charismatic

People think it means – A person with a great personality.

What it means in church – A person who sometimes talks in a funny language and waves his arms a lot, and may or may not have a great personality.

Come Forward

People think it means – To fess up or admit that you know something.

What it means in church – To fess up and admit that you don't know anything.

Devotions

People think it means – Bible reading and prayers done by super-spiritual people.

What it means in church – Bible reading and prayers done by ordinary people.

Eternity

People think it means – An expensive fragrance from Calvin Klein.

What it means in church – The eternal life after this one, where you won't need any fragrances.

Evangelist

People think it means – A flamboyant person with unusual clothing and a unique hairstyle.

What it means in church – A flamboyant person with unusual clothing and a unique hairstyle.

Freedom in Christ

People think it means – That you are free to do anything you want.

What it means in church – That you are free to do anything God wants.

Glory

People think it means – When someone wants all the attention.

What it means in church – When God wants all the attention. Also, an expression of amazement accompanied by hand waving, as in "Glory!"

Grace

People think it means – Something you say before a meal; the blessing.

What it means in church - A blessing from God that we don't deserve.

Hymns, Hymnal

People think it means – A dusty book full of old songs nobody sings anymore.

What it means in church – A dusty book full of old songs that your parents sang. This definition has applied to every generation since the beginning of music.

Lay Person

People think it means – A person caught sleeping on the job.

What it means in church – Any nonpaid church member caught sleeping in church.

Legalism

People think it means – The act of following the rule of law.

What it means in church – Trying to win brownie points with God by working real hard in church and then complaining that nobody seems to notice.

Lift Up Your Hands

People think it means – Wanting to be called on by the teacher.

What it means in church – Wanting to be called on by God.

Missionary Barrel

People think it means – Something rough and itchy worn by missionaries.

What it means in church – An actual barrel containing rough and itchy worn clothing intended for missionaries.

New Life

People think it means – Getting a second chance after faltering.

What it means in church – Getting a second chance after faltering.

Offering, Offertory

People think it means – A special time during the church service when people are forced to give money, followed by an amateurish musical number.

What it means in church – A special time during the church service when people willingly give money, followed by an amateurish musical number.

Prayer

People think it means – When someone doesn't have a chance, as in "He doesn't have a prayer."

What it means in church – What all people engage in when they don't think they have a prayer.

Responsive Reading

People think it means – A certain kind of book that encourages discussion.

What it means in church – A certain kind of text you read in church because the bulletin tells you to.

Saved

People think it means – Your old life is spared because someone helped you.

What it means in church – You are given new life because God reached out to you.

Sin, Sinner

People think it means – A mistake or an error; a sinner is someone who makes mistakes but doesn't really mean to.

What it means in church – An offense to God; a sinner is someone who has offended God by choice.

Spiritual

People think it means – That inner part of your being that's connected to the great cosmic consciousness.

What it means in church – That part of your nature that lives forever; the part that God changes when you're saved.

Testimony

People think it means – Telling the truth in front of a judge and jury.

What it means in church – Telling the truth about God in front of anybody who will listen.

Tithes

People think it means – A certain kind of neckwear worn by men in church.

What it means in church – The amount of money that people think they should give to God (only they never give this much).

Tract

People think it means – A large number of homes that all look alike.

What it means in church – A flyer or booklet that explains how to be saved.

Worldly

People think it means – A person who is wise to the ways of the world, which is a positive quality if you want to get ahead in life.

What it means in church – A person who is wise to the ways of the world, which is great in this life, but won't do you a whole lot of good in eternity.

CHAPTER 7

How to Know When You Are Ready to Join a Church

Some people avoid becoming a member of a church due to indecision or a fear of commitment. Fear of commitment is probably a spiritual problem that is outside the scope of this manual. But we can help people who can't decide whether or not they should join a church.

Here are the top seven clues that will reveal if you are ready to become a member of the church you are attending:

① The cushion of your favorite pew or chair has a permanent impression that matches the contour of your rear end.

② You are so familiar with the other people in the church that you know everyone's "unspoken" prayer requests.

③ There is a large oil stain at your favorite spot in the church parking lot. The configuration of the stain matches the one in your own garage.

④ You don't take your Bible home after church each
Sunday. To avoid lugging it back and forth each week,
you just hide it behind the plastic ficus tree in the
church foyer at the end of the church service. You
retrieve it the next week before you enter the sanctuary.

⑤ You got tired of writing a note on the back of the registration card each week with your constructive criticism to improve the worship service. So you special-
ordered a rubber stamp. Now, each week, you simply
imprint the back of your registration card with your
I DON'T LIKE THE MUSIC stamp.

⑥ Most of the punch stains on the carpet in the
Fellowship Hall were caused by you.

⑦ You have the numbers for the deacons and your pastor
on your telephone's speed dial.

When you are ready to
join the church, you will
become part of a
church membership
class such as this one.
Like the church body,
the membership class
includes a diversity of
people, fashion sense,
and eyeglass styles.

CHAPTER 8

How to Really Worship God

It's easy to find humor in the people and practices of the church. Every culture has its peculiarities and "inside jokes," and the church—which is the largest culture on the planet—is no different. There's a lot of stuff that must seem a little strange to those who aren't in the church culture. Hey, there's stuff that sometimes seems peculiar to those of us who go to church, and we're used to it!

In fact, the Bible refers to Christians as a "peculiar people" who have been called by God "out of darkness into his marvellous light" (1 Peter 2:9 KJV). That doesn't mean that you're strange if you go to church. In this context, "peculiar" means you are special. More specifically, being peculiar in church means you are special to God, who has called you to show others His goodness and worthiness.

If you have ever wondered why there's such a thing as church in the first place, this is it. Church isn't a private club where members go to perform sacred rituals. It isn't a building where people who think they're better than everyone else go to hang out. Church is a living organism—a body of believers—designed by God to show His light to a dark world. When we worship God together in church, it's like we are saying to the world: "This is who God is, and He is worthy to receive all the honor and praise we can possibly give Him."

When it's working the way God designed it, the church is like a lighthouse, and when we worship God in church through our singing, through the preaching, and even through our giving, it's like we are turning on a big bright light that shows everyone how great and how good God is.

It's true that we can't see God, but we can see His light and His love. And the more we learn about God and what He does for us, the better we can worship Him.

> *But the time is coming and is already here when true worshipers will worship the Father in spirit and in truth. The Father is looking for anyone who will worship him that way.*
>
> JOHN 4:23

CHAPTER 9

How to Tell the Difference Between a Deacon and a Trustee

It is relatively easy to identify those people who are employed by your church. Certain members of the church staff are immediately recognizable because of their distinctive appearance or function:

The *Senior Pastor* is the guy standing at the front door of the church with his Bible tucked under his armpit as he smiles and shakes hands with people exiting from the sanctuary on Sunday morning.

The *Youth Pastor* is always wearing sunglasses (especially indoors) and usually isn't wearing socks (especially with dress slacks and shoes).

The *Church Secretary* looks frazzled, nervous, and exhausted. From her appearance, you would think that she is the hardest working person on the church staff. You'd be right.

But there are lots of people who work at the church who aren't on the payroll. These are called "lay people." That means that they have real jobs in the outside world, but they take on considerable work at the church for free.

The derivation of the term *lay person* reflects the progression of their involvement: They were laying around doing nothing until one day when they volunteered to help; ever since, the church staff has been laying a load of responsibilities on them.

Lay people fulfill many vital roles around the church. Most of the time, you can't tell which lay person does what, unless you catch them in action. They all look similar to each other—just like regular folks. Although lay people may not be distinguishable by their appearance, don't make the mistake of thinking that all lay people are the same. Their roles (referred to as lay ministries) differ significantly and should not be confused.

Perhaps the greatest division between lay roles exists with deacons and trustees. An entire subculture of lay ministry is built upon the distinction between these two roles. Basically, the difference is quite simple:

Deacons: These are the servants of the church. They take care of the practical needs of the church members. They make sure that meals are delivered to the sick, that people are visited in the hospital, and that home repairs are handled for the elderly.

Trustees: These are the financial protectors of the church. They are in charge of the money and how it is spent. Because buildings often represent the church's most valuable investment, they often oversee the use of the facilities.

You might think that these two lay ministries could work together in peaceful coexistence. Nothing could be farther from the truth. There is a dynamic tension that comes into play as each group vies for more influence. Each group thinks that their ministry is more vital to the church, so the trustees and deacons compete against each other for power and prestige and the distinction of superior humility.

Both the trustees and the deacons are constantly attempting to forge strategic alliances with unsuspecting church members. You must be forewarned and adequately equipped to distinguish between the deacons and the trustees. Since they will look alike to the casual observer, you must pay close attention to what they say. Only by their words can you distinguish them.

Deacons say things like:

- It is our pleasure to serve you.
- Let us assist you with that.
- Please don't hesitate to call us if we can be of further help.
- Jesus cared for others, and so do we.

It's easy to tell the difference between a deacon and a trustee simply by observing what they do at church events. Here's Ed at the annual church picnic. Notice that he is picking up the dishes and trash others have left behind. Clearly Ed is a deacon. Of course, from the expression on his face, you can tell that on this particular occasion he would much rather be a trustee.

Trustees say things like:

- Who do you think is going to pay for that?

- There would be less wear and tear on the sanctuary carpet if we held the worship services in the parking lot.

- People pay big bucks to see a movie. Perhaps we should impose an admission charge on Sunday morning.

- Jesus didn't spend a lot of money, and neither will we.

Don't get the impression that the deacons are saintly and the trustees are cursed. The deacons have an unfair advantage when it comes to public perception: It is their job to help people. Everybody loves a servant. On the other hand, the trustees carry the heavy burden of making sure that the church budget stays in balance. They have the unpopular job of saying "no" to the frequent monetary requests of the various ministries. Nobody likes a Scrooge, but it is the trustee's job to fulfill that role for the sake of the church's fiscal well-being. After all, money is usually very tight. Most churches don't have sufficient funds to pay the youth pastor enough salary to afford a pair of socks.

CHAPTER 10

How to Deal with Someone Who Sits in Your Pew

Human beings are by nature territorial. Whether it's your house or apartment, your office cubicle, your notebook computer, or your personalized coffee mug, you own or use certain things and spaces that you like to think belong exclusively to you. This sense of territorial ownership even extends to places and objects that belong to no one in particular, but you claim them as your own because you occupy or use them on a regular basis. These are things like a certain parking space at work, a table at your favorite restaurant, a comfortable chair in your family room, or a particular pew at church. Other people may use these things when you're not around, but when you are, they better be available for you and you alone.

For the purposes of this church-case scenario book, let's talk about that place in church where you sit every Sunday morning. If you go to a traditional church, it's probably a pew, or at least a portion of a pew, probably on the aisle, not too close to the front, but not too far back, either. If you go to a church where people sit on chairs instead of padded oak pews, it's no different. You have a spot where you like to sit. It's yours. People know it. The ushers know it. The pastor knows it. You don't want to have to clutter your mind with thoughts of "Where am I going to sit this morning?" as you get ready for church. You want to walk into church with your mind focused on the Lord. You don't want to have to deal with some upstart sitting in your pew.

But it's bound to happen. At some point in your church experience someone is going to break the unwritten code of conduct and sit where you always sit. One of the ushers is going to drop the ball and let a whole family occupy your space. And there you'll be, walking into church with nothing to think about except staying awake, and you'll see someone sitting in your pew. What can you do about it?

① **You can quietly complain to the head usher.**
Since one of the ushers didn't prevent the problem, you can express your disappointment to the usher in charge. However, this won't help the reputation you are trying to develop as someone who serves others.

② **You can ask the person in your pew to move.**
This is an option, but it could prove to be embarrassing, both for you and for the person in your pew. No one likes to create a "scene," especially in church

on Sunday morning, and this is exactly what will happen, especially when the pew poacher—who is considerably larger than you—resists and says to you, "I don't see your name on this pew."

Most dedicated pew sitters are the same at home as they are at church. In this photo you can see Willard in his favorite chair, which no one else in his family has ever occupied.

③ **You can put your name on the pew.**

Borrow a technique used by football stadiums and basketball arenas. When a wealthy patron purchases a "Personal Seat License," the name of the person is inscribed on a brass plate and then bolted to the back of the chair. You could be the first in your church to purchase a "Personal Pew License."

However, this would clearly put you at odds with Scripture, which says:

> *If you give special attention and a good*
> *seat to the rich person, but you say to the poor one,*
> *"You can stand over there, or else sit on the floor"—*
> *well, doesn't this discrimination show that you*
> *are guided by wrong motives?*
>
> JAMES 2:3–4

④ **You can get to your pew before anyone else.**
This requires that you "camp out" in your seat long before everyone else arrives, making sure that you and you alone occupy your pew. The upside of this technique is that you can use the extra time to read your Bible, creating the impression that you are very spiritual. The downside is that most people—your own family in particular—will see through your charade and start spreading the truth about your pew obsession.

⑤ **You can relax and let others have the best seats in the church.**
While this may take some time for you to get used to, this is probably the best alternative to dealing with someone who sits in your pew. Just make sure you don't fall in love with an entirely new pew.

CHAPTER 11

How to Handle a Hypocrite

The dictionary defines a *hypocrite* as a person who pretends to be what he or she is not. In the church-case scenario, the hypocrites are the ones who pretend to be super saintly when they are just as sinful as the rest of the congregation. Unfortunately, there are lots of hypocrites in every church. But don't let that dissuade you from attending—there is always room for one more. Yes, you get our point. We are all hypocrites to one degree or another. Especially on Sundays. Even though we can't hide our weaknesses from God, we do our best to camouflage them from the other folks at church.

While we all suffer from momentary outbreaks of phoniness, you will find several individuals in the church who excel at such insincerity.

Matt, the high school kid who leads the youth group Bible study: At school he spends his time in the computer lab manipulating digital images of his teachers for purposes of extorting lunch money from them.

Janet, the fourth-grade Sunday school teacher: She owns and operates a tattoo parlor in nearby Springfield under the name of "Satanic Skin Graphics."

Richard, the head usher: He was the real-life inspiration for "Norm" on the *Cheers* television series. He is a daily patron at The Elbow Room in the sleazy part of town. How ironic that his favorite hymn is "Fill My Cup, Lord."

It's as if the church hypocrites are living in two worlds: Their "church life" is totally separate and distinct from their "real world." Often their "real world" behavior isn't any worse than how the rest of us behave. What makes them intolerable is their saintly performance each Sunday, accompanied by a condescending and judgmental attitude. Self-promoting testimonies of their virtuous behavior are particularly nauseating because they usually condemn the sinful behavior in which they excel.

Handling a hypocrite is a delicate matter. Your first tendency will be to stuff a church bulletin down his or her holy yap hole when they emit one of their sanctimonious prayers. (If you do it fast enough, the secrecy of your identity can be preserved since everyone will have their eyes closed.) Actually, the ancient history of the Christian church includes some beheadings and the occasional burning at the stake as punishments for alleged hypocrites. Unfortunately, it is the modern view that sadistic torture, as satisfying as it may be, is not an acceptable form of church discipline. You are going to have to be content with some type of nonviolent method of dealing with the hypocrites in your church.

We suggest the simple yet effective method of public

humiliation. Catch the hypocrite in an act of deceit, and then publicize the event. For purposes of illustration, we will use the hypothetical examples given above:

① **How to deal with Matt:**

Someone in the youth group should suggest holding an on-campus Bible study in the high school computer lab. While one of the kids is yawning, he can accidentally hit Matt's keyboard to reveal his despicable handiwork. (If this approach doesn't work, then you may have to resort to serving a subpoena on several of the teachers, forcing them to testify before the State Board of Education.)

② **How to deal with Janet:**

Someone from your church will need to move to Springfield and join the Chamber of Commerce. That person can then nominate Satanic Skin Graphics for "business of the year." The local newspaper will cover the event and report a story on all of the nominees. Plan to distribute copies of that issue of the *Springfield Gazette* in all of the hymnal racks in your church.

③ **How to deal with Richard:**

Plan an event for your church during which time

members will pass out evangelistic leaflets ("tracts") on skid row every Saturday night. Station church members at strategic locations for maximum witnessing visibility. Perhaps you could assign the pastor and his wife to stand at the doorway of The Elbow Room.

Ridding your church of a self-righteous hypocrite requires discipline and diligence on your part. You must always be prepared. Carry a miniature tape recorder and pocket-sized camera with you at all times. You never know when your target may slip up and display his or her true nature at church. That is what happened to Chad. At church he was the holier-than-thou president of the choir; at work, however, Chad was the office womanizer. Thanks to the quick thinking and fast shutter snapping of a member of the choir, Chad's double life was exposed at the church choir's winter retreat. As the photograph on the following page reveals, Chad was caught trying to pick up a single woman from the soprano section while everyone else was praying.

Dealing with a hypocrite also involves restoration after a sufficient period of public humiliation. The true-life story of Chad is a good example of how a hypocrite can be reinstated to usefulness in the church. The shame of that picture caused Chad to resign as president. Shortly thereafter, he dropped

out of the choir altogether. But the pastoral staff didn't want Chad to be totally alienated from the church. They went to great lengths to find a suitable ministry for him. Currently he has the task of scraping dried chewing gum off the undersides of the pews. This ministry serves a dual purpose: It promotes sanitation within the church and serves as a deterrent to other would-be hypocrites.

CHAPTER 12

How to Respond When Church Gossip Hits Home

Any way you look at it, there's no way to put a positive spin on gossip. Oh, gossip may help make you feel better (temporarily), but it doesn't help the person you're talking about. By definition, *gossip* is talk that involves the personal matters—true or false—of other people. Not coincidentally, the person who engages in such conversation is called a *gossip*. Of course, that's only when people talk outside of church. Once they enter church property or engage in church activities, gossip turns into something much more spiritual. We give it different names, but it's still gossip:

Sharing Time. This can be a structured time during a small group meeting or Bible study, or it can be an informal time before, during, or after church. The gossip couches the news in a concerned tone of voice known as "sharing," as in, "I'd like to share with you a concern I have about Jack." Only Jack isn't there and probably has no idea that someone is sharing his personal matters with other people.

Tip: When engaged in sharing time, it helps to hold your Bible in front of you, grasping it with your right arm to your chest as you gesture with your left arm. This gives you an extra measure of spiritual credibility.

Prayer Time. This is a subtler version of sharing time. Prayer time usually occurs just before a small group, such as a Sunday school class or a Bible study, begins the actual lesson or study. After everyone has had a chance to get coffee and snacks, a group leader will ask if anyone has a prayer need or a prayer request. The gossip will spill the personal news in this way: "I'd like to ask for prayer for Jill, who is experiencing some difficulties right now." Everyone else will nod in agreement, except for Jill, who isn't at the prayer time.

Tip: Gossip veterans know that you don't give the juicy details until the prayer actually begins. Since you are "talking to God," you can disguise the gossip as a prayer, and since you're praying for Jill rather than talking about her, you can spill the beans without appearing to take any delight in her unfortunate situation.

The Prayer Chain. This is a clever variation on the chain letter or chain E-mail, only it involves the phone. Prayer chains are set up in advance by a particular church group to quickly spread gossip—er, prayer requests—by calling people with information about individuals or families who are having a rough time. If you are in the prayer chain and you receive such a call, it is then your job to call the next person on the list of prayer chain participants. The advantage of the prayer chain is that news can travel faster than a prairie fire. The disadvantage is that the message sometimes gets distorted as it passes from one person to another. Of course, gossip is based on distortion, so it's no big deal.

Tip: If you are part of a prayer chain and don't want to miss out, be sure to add the "call forwarding" feature to your phone. That way you will be sure to know everything that's going on.

With all the benefits of disguising gossip in spiritual terms, there is a downside. Without your knowledge, you could be on the other end of a prayer request or a prayer chain. In other words, you could be the object rather than the initiator of gossip. There is a chance that the people praying for you are completely sincere and have a genuine concern for your well-being, but just in case they aren't, it's a good idea to do some praying of your own. Only don't tell anyone. Keep it between you and God.

How to Support a Missionary Family

Most church members are very glad to contribute financial support toward a missionary family. For a relatively small cost, they can avoid the guilt of not being missionaries themselves. And therein lies the problem. In most church-case scenarios, the financial support for missionaries is too small.

Look at this picture of a typical missionary family. You might immediately assume that this is an old photograph from the 1960s. You would be wrong. This is a very recent

Yours in the Fellowship of His Service . . . The Nelsons

photograph of a missionary family from Brazil. Actually, Jim and Sue Nelson are a stylish couple, and their children are as fashion-conscious as other kids their age. But the Nelsons look old-fashioned because they have been forced to suffer the indignity of living out of the *missionary barrel.*

Most churches have a missionary barrel for collecting things that members don't want anymore. But the church members don't want to discard these worn items without getting a charitable tax deduction. So they pitch their unwanted goods into a large receptacle (customarily located in the church's janitorial closet). The items in the barrel are wrapped as Christmas gifts and shipped overseas to various missionary families in November (usually arriving in February).

Most missionaries have not taken a vow of poverty. They just look that way because they only get stuff from the missionary barrel. But that is no way to treat missionaries. Proper care and support of a missionary family consists of these five simple rules:

(1) **Forget the missionary barrel. Send cash.**

Don't worry that the missionary family will spend the money frivolously. It is difficult to be extravagant in a third-world country when there are no indoor toilets or shopping malls.

(2) **Don't send supplies that you have already used.**
Yes, there is still life left in a tea bag that has only
been used once, but you shouldn't collect them and
send them to the missionaries. If you don't want to
use them anymore, throw them away. What makes
you think that the missionaries will enjoy recycling
your once-used tea bag in their cup of hot water? The
same principle applies to other used items. They don't
want to give their child a coloring book that has most
of the pages already colored on by your kid. And we
shouldn't even have to explain the hygienic reasons for
not sending slightly used Kleenex.

(3) **Don't send clothes that you have already worn.**
It doesn't matter that those clothes were in style
when you purchased them twelve years ago. They
aren't now. That's why you don't wear them anymore.
Well, that's the same reason the missionaries don't
want to wear them, either. Sure, the indigenous
inhabitants of the Gobi desert may not be as fashion
savvy as you are, but the missionaries know what is
in style. They get current magazines and log onto the
Internet. They know what is in fashion (and that
your used clothes are not). When they send a family
picture to the churches back home, they don't want
to be looking like *the Nelsons.*

④ **Don't send them any new clothes that you wouldn't wear yourself.**

This is a variation on Rule #3. This applies to new clothes that you might purchase for the missionary Christmas gifts. Don't try to save a few cents by shopping stores that only sell merchandise that has been discontinued, damaged, or flawed. And resist the temptation to make your purchase at any store that has the word "irregular" in its name.

⑤ **When they come home on furlough, don't treat your missionaries like vagabonds.**

The beds in the church nursery are great for infants, but the teenage children of the missionary family shouldn't have to sleep in them. Sleeping bags on the floor of the church kitchen aren't acceptable, either. Go wild and let your missionaries stay in a nice hotel. If your church can't afford a hotel, let them stay in your home. (Give them your bedroom, not a cot on the front porch.)

There might be resistance to abandoning the use of the missionary barrel in your church. If this happens, take a church vote. Make the people who vote in favor of the barrel wear the clothes that are contained therein. Make sure you have a camera ready.

CHAPTER 14

How to Love Everybody in Church

Remember all that stuff in Chapter 8 about peculiar church people and how it means *special* rather than *strange*? Well, in God's eyes you may be special, but to everyone else you are a little strange. Because of this, you are sometimes hard to love (collective gasp), even for your fellow churchgoers.

As hard as that is to believe, you might as well face it. There are times when you are downright unlovable. It doesn't matter that God loves you unconditionally. People around you (including your own family) put conditions on their love for you, and you do the same to them.

The reason for this conditional love should be quite obvious. We tend to love the lovable, and we don't really care for the person who sits in our spot, the people we consider to be phony, or the person who spreads gossip about us. Of course, other people have a hard time loving us for the same reasons. In other words, we're all in the same boat. We live by the motto: "You can't love all of the people all of the time, so you may as well love some of the people some of the time."

There's only one problem with that motto. God's not

real fond of it. He didn't design the church only for the lovely or the lovable (if He did, there wouldn't be a single member). To the contrary, God established the church to break down the walls of prejudice, hostility, and irritation that naturally keep us apart. Knowing that we couldn't do this on our own, God did something truly amazing. He showed us how to love each other by loving us first.

> *God showed how much he loved us by sending his only Son into the world so that we might have eternal life through him. This is real love. It is not that we loved God, but that he loved us and sent his Son as a sacrifice to take away our sins. Dear friends, since God loved us that much, we surely ought to love each other.*
>
> 1 JOHN 4:9–11

CHAPTER 15

How to Get Elected to the Church Board

What can you do if you want to be an elected public servant but you are also a Christian? You can't go into the world of politics. It is oxymoronic to envision yourself as a Christian politician. But don't despair. You need not abandon your dream of eloquent campaign speeches and election-night jitters. Within the church-case scenario, you can run for election to the church board.

Church board elections are slightly different than public elections. There are usually no campaign placards or slogans plastered on the walls of the sanctuary. For some reason, churches consider election banners to be unseemly. "Vote for Steve Kampsen—He's the anti-sin candidate" has a nice ring to it, but you'll never see it on a sanctuary wall.

Because you'll be prohibited from the use of campaign publicity, it is all the more important that you adhere to the following rules:

(1) **Avoid giving the impression that you are an independent thinker.**

Nobody wants this kind of person on the board.

People want you to vote their way, whether you like it or not.

(2) **But don't let them think that you are brain-dead.**
A person in that condition only qualifies to be the sponsor of the junior high youth group.

(3) **Don't appear to be too young.**
The church board is no place for inexperience.

(4) **But don't look too old.**
Church traditions are honored, but you can't appear to be intolerant of new ideas. The current board members probably look like contemporaries of Elijah. Let the voters think that you are young enough bring the church out of the Old Testament era (which gives you latitude to look as old as the apostle Paul or John the Baptist).

(5) **Don't come across as aloof.**
You've got to present yourself as "one of the people" if you are going to have any hope of gaining power over them.

(6) **But don't be too friendly.**
People will assume that you are trying to schmooze your way onto the board.

⑦ **Avoid any appearance of wealth.**
You don't want to be labeled as *worldly* or *materialistic.* How much is too much? This is a difficult question. It is usually a matter of personal subjectivity. You have to be perceived as earning slightly less than the people who are voting for you.

⑧ **But don't let them think that you are unsuccessful.**
If you can't make your own business profitable, you won't be entrusted with the church's fiscal responsibilities, such as determining whether members of the senior adult group should pay twenty-seven cents per mile or thirty-one cents per mile for use of the church bus.

Let these eight rules be your guidelines. You may need to adjust or refine them depending on the peculiarities of your own church. There is one general rule, however, that is universally applicable to every church: Blend in. If you stand out from the crowd, you won't get elected. For the most part, church board members are generic. So fit into the mold.

The photograph on the next page depicts six typical board candidates. In an effort to preserve the dignity of these naïve candidates, we have anonymously labeled them as Candidates A, B, C, D, E, and F (moving from left to right). Even if you ignore the eight guidelines, you should be able to assess the viability of each candidate by applying only the "blend in" principle.

Candidates C and F: These guys are eliminated at the outset. Their suits aren't dark enough. Everyone knows that spiritual people only wear dark clothing. These two candidates are wearing suits more appropriate for Mark Twain than a church board member.

Candidate A: This guy has only got it half right (the upper half). Maybe he could garner a few votes if the candidates were seated at a table so his trousers didn't show. We can only guess that he was trying to capture the youth vote with his radical appearance. But he made a fatal rookie mistake. No one without liver spots ever votes for the church board members.

Candidates D and E: These guys will get elected. They have achieved the bland appearance that church members are comfortable with.

Candidate B: This guy will be elected as chairman of the church board. He is bland, yet that flower on his lapel gives him a hint of style. (Actually, he is totally lacking in style. His wife put the flower on his lapel so she could distinguish him from Candidates D and E.)

If you don't think that you can capture the votes from a sufficient number of church members, you will have to extend your timetable and alter your techniques. Start bringing doughnuts to church (preferably Krispy Kremes). Distribute them without charge every Sunday after the worship service. Only place your name in nomination for the church board if you have been bringing doughnuts for three years. Let the word leak out that you are likely to change churches if you aren't elected to the board. It is devious, but it is your only hope if you don't own a dark suit.

CHAPTER 16

How to Break Up a Fight in a Church Board Meeting

For the most part the church board serves a very useful function. Like any good company board, a church board helps keep everyone focused on the purpose and the mission statement of the organization. Most church boards function effectively when the issues involve strategies for the spiritual development of the staff and church members. It's always exciting to discuss programs that encourage personal and congregational growth.

However, there are some issues that tend to cause infighting and ultimately divide church boards. You would think these issues would concern church beliefs and practices, but that is rarely the case. The truth is that church boards tend to fight over much more mundane issues, such as the color of the new carpet in the sanctuary or the flavor of the punch at church socials. You would think that members of the church board, who are elected or appointed on the basis of their spiritual maturity, would be above some petty differences. You would think that they would strive together to preserve the unity of the "body." That has been known to happen, but very often the church board is far from united.

What can be done to bring harmony to your church board? How do you stop the infighting? Here are several church-case scenarios:

① **Get elected to the church board.**

It's hard to break up a fight between board members unless you are one of them. See Chapter 15 for instructions on getting elected to the church board.

② **Lay low for the first few meetings.**

Don't say anything for at least six meetings. It's important that you don't just sit there with a sleepy, disinterested expression on your face. During the board meeting, take notes on a yellow legal pad, look at each person who speaks, and nod your head in approval while thoughtfully stroking your chin. But never speak. Memorize this saying: "Better to keep your mouth shut and make people wonder if you're wise than to open your mouth and remove all doubt."

③ **Choose your words carefully.**

After an appropriate time of silence, begin speaking at board meetings, but not too much. Keep in mind that it's better to ask questions than to make statements.

Continuing with the thoughtful chin-stroking technique, ask questions such as:

- "Are you sure we want to do that?"

- "What is the upside potential?"

- "What is the downside potential?"

- "Have we considered all of the alternatives?"

- "Do you want my people to look into it?"

Even though you don't have any answers or "people," other board members will be intrigued by your questions, and one or two of them may begin to wonder if, in fact, you are important enough to have people.

④ **Don't choose sides.**
If your goal is to be the peacemaker on the church board, it's very important not to choose sides. Become an expert at using the phrases "On the one hand" and "On the other hand."

⑤ **Step forward when needed.**
Once you have gained the confidence and respect of your peers, you are now ready to step forward when a church board fight breaks out. Because you are the

Switzerland of board members—neutral and in the middle—you will be in the best position to prevent infighting. Your best tools for preventing an all-out board war and restoring harmony will be a few well-turned phrases. As much as possible, use Bible verses and, if needed, the wise sayings of Ben Franklin. Don't worry about mixing these up. Most people can't tell the difference between Scripture and *Poor Richard's Almanack*. Here are some examples:

- "How wonderful it is, how pleasant, when brothers live together in harmony!"
- "God helps those who help themselves."
- "Blessed are the meek, for they shall inherit the earth."
- "Do unto others as you would have them do unto you."
- "Submit to one another out of reverence to Christ."
- "Don't count your chickens before they hatch."

All of the aforementioned questions and phrases can be used interchangeably and in various combinations. You won't actually be contributing to the development of the board, but you will be credited with keeping it together. And in the end, isn't harmony more important than progress?

CHAPTER 17

How to Join the Church Choir
(When You Don't Know How to Sing)

There are certain benefits available to members of the church choir:

You get preferred seating at each worship service. Better than being in the front row, most churches have a "choir loft" consisting of a special arrangement of chairs on the stage reserved for choir members only.

You can cut out of Sunday school class early. No one will question you if they think you are leaving early because the choir needs to rehearse the anthem one more time before the worship service starts. This "escape clause" allows you to drive to Starbucks between Sunday school and the worship service.

You don't have to worry about getting dressed up for church. You can be as sloppy as you want to be. Those choir robes hide everything.

You don't have to diet. Even though you stand in front

of the congregation each week, you can put on a few extra pounds and no one will suspect anything. Those choir robes really do hide everything.

Perhaps you have been interested in joining the choir, but you considered your chances to be bleak because you can't sing. That's no problem. Vocal ability is not a prerequisite for most choirs. (You must not have listened to many church choirs or else you would have known better.)

The primary consideration for choir membership is appearance. Don't let this factor intimidate you. Remember, we are only talking about appearance from the neck up (thanks again to those choir robes). Here are the criteria you must satisfy:

① **You must have hair that lies relatively flat against your head.**

A "pouf" radius of two inches is allowed around the circumference of your skull. A hairstyle any wider than two inches will block the choir director's view of the people standing behind you. (Exceptions are allowed for anyone who sings bass. The bass section always stands in the back row, so a bouffant hairstyle won't block anyone. Unfortunately, bass singers are usually bald men, and they don't need to rely on the exception.)

② **You must have impeccable dental hygiene.**
Nothing is worse than random food particles stuck
in the teeth of a wide-mouthed soprano.

③ **You must have the ability to read and move your lips
at the same time.**
If you can't sing, then you'll need to fake it. Most
choirs sing from sheet music and don't memorize the
words. You'll need to be able to "mouth" the words in

Sometimes choir members
with vocal abilities
are bothered by
those members who
can't sing a note.
Cheryl, Susan, and
Glenda have great
voices. They were
patient for a long
time, but they finally
seceded from the
choir and formed
their own trio. These
gals, who bill them-
selves as The
Angelic Voices,
are available to
perform at Sunday
services, revivals,
retreats, and
"singspirations."

an animated fashion as you read along to give the appearance that you are singing. (Note: Persons who are accustomed to speed-reading may have difficulty with this maneuver.)

④ **You must be able to stay awake during boring sermons.**

The job security of the choir director is in jeopardy if a choir member falls asleep during the pastor's sermon. (Don't let this job qualification discourage you from applying for the choir. If you tend to be a worship service snoozer, read Chapter 5.)

Of course, there must be a few people in the choir who can actually carry a tune. But only a few of those are necessary. A good sound technician can work wonders with the correct amplifiers and modulators. The one thing that can't be faked is the number of people in the choir. And that's where you come in. A large choir is the sign of a healthy church. So your church choir director won't care that you are tone-deaf if you are willing to occupy a chair in the choir loft.

All the benefits of choir membership can be yours if you are willing to expend just a little effort. All it takes is for you to sign up and then shut up.

CHAPTER 18

How to Know When You're Ready to Sing a Solo

It's one thing to sing in the choir. As we learned in the last chapter, being able to sing on key and harmonize with your fellow singers isn't nearly as important as showing up for rehearsal and smiling brightly when the choir sings on Sunday morning. But singing a solo in front of the church congregation—now that's an entirely different matter.

Not just anybody has that rare combination of amateur ability and raw nerve to stand in front of a church full of people and sing all four verses of "How Great Thou Art," especially when the accompaniment consists of a weekend piano player and an organist who is more comfortable playing in a baseball park than a church.

But if you think you have what it takes and you think you're ready to step away from the choir and move up to the level of star performer on Sunday morning, then here are a few indicators that will tell you when you're ready to go solo:

① You know the proper hand gestures, including the correct way to hold a microphone.

Since you probably won't be able to hold an audience spellbound with your incredible voice (don't feel bad, few people can), your best asset will be the way you use your hands to distract the audience from your voice. Study the movements of seasoned gospel music performers. Most of them can't sing a lick, and yet many of them have built impressive careers simply by mesmerizing audiences with the movement of their hands during a song. In addition to watching their expressive hands, notice how they handle the microphone—skillfully holding it at arm's length for those dramatic high notes and at close range for those quiet low notes. A good soloist will work the microphone like a trombone player at a John Philip Sousa festival.

(2) **You wear the correct outfit and have the latest hairstyle.**

Another good way to distract from your singing is to wear the correct wardrobe and sport the latest gospel music hairstyle. There's nothing like a flashy dress or a loud plaid sport coat to cover up any flaws in your singing. In addition to clothing, a poufy hairdo (for the ladies) or a radical comb over (for the men) will transfix your audience.

As an example, we offer the three ladies in the

photo below. None of these women is ready to go solo, which is why they're practicing a song arranged for a ladies' trio. Notice their outfits. The singer on the left is just too plain. There's no drama in the dress. The singer on the right is out of style, and her facial expression shows how uncomfortable she is. The singer in the center has the best shot at going solo. She has a nifty hairdo, her dress is quite fashionable, and she already knows that a seasoned soloist never holds the sheet music. Actually, the piano player probably has the best chance of launching a church solo career. Her hair is the poufiest of all, and that blouse and belt are pretty loud.

If you can't sing, you haven't yet mastered the hand gestures, and you don't have that gospel music fashion sense, don't give up hope. There is one more way to get on the solo circuit.

③ **You are really good at singing to prerecorded background instrumental music.**

What we're talking about here is a form of karaoke (only without the drinking). The idea is that the soloist sings the lyrics while a tape machine plays the instrumental accompaniment. Few people realize that this popular form of entertainment originated in the church, and not in Japanese sushi bars. Back in the early 1980s, when the cassette tape officially replaced the eight-track as the music format of choice, someone got the bright idea to record the instrumental track to all of your favorite hymns and gospel songs. For the first time, aspiring soloists could sound like they had the backing of Nashville's finest musicians as they belted out their favorite tunes.

Now it really didn't matter how bad they sounded. A creative instrumental tape could easily overshadow a poor solo performance. (If you doubt what we're saying, imagine what Willie Nelson would sound like without any of those highly paid musicians backing him up.)

The only problem is that not everyone can sing to a background instrumental track. It takes practice and timing to get all of the nuances right. You've got to sound like the prerecorded orchestra is following you rather than the other way around, and you've got to make sure that the high school kid who runs the sound system in your church isn't asleep at the switch when you're ready to start your song. There's nothing worse than standing on stage all by yourself, microphone in hand, with nothing but a nervous smile and a narrow gaze directed at the sound booth, where "Rocky" frantically fumbles for the start button on the tape player.

If you can solve all of these problems—and you've feel like you've been called to go solo—then we suggest you go for it. What's the worst that could happen? Even if you don't succeed, you'll have a closet full of crazy outfits and a heart full of memories.

CHAPTER 19

How a Church Finds a Pastor

From time to time in the life of every church, it becomes necessary to fill the position of Senior Pastor. Hiring a pastor isn't as easy as hiring a greeter for Wal-Mart (although there are similarities between the two jobs). You just can't advertise in the classifieds of the local newspaper. That's not how churches work.

The procedure for finding a pastor usually involves a prolonged and structured process:

1. **Form a Pastor Search Committee.**

   This isn't as easy as it seems. There should only be a few committee members to ensure confidentiality of the group's discussions. (In most churches, public dissemination of information increases in direct proportion to the number of people who promise to keep the information confidential.) On the other hand, the committee must reflect a broad cross section of the congregation and all of the church's constituencies. The solution is to select at least one committee member who is involved in lots of church activities at the same time; this one member can serve as the token representative for each of those groups. The ideal member will be:

- a board member,
- who teaches Sunday school,
- sings in the choir,
- works with the youth group,
- serves as an alternate usher (whenever there is a fifth Sunday in a month),
- volunteers in the church nursery during the worship service,
- co-chairs the kitchen cleanup committee,
- serves on the Foreign Missions Committee, and
- leads the Visitation Team that makes house calls every Monday night to the first-time visitors who attended the church the prior Sunday.

With this one individual, you've got most of the ministries of the church represented on the Pastor Search Committee.

② **Schedule regular, clandestine meetings of the committee.**

The committee will need to meet regularly if it is to accomplish its task within a reasonable time frame. Therefore, the committee should plan to meet weekly. Because confidentiality (which is the spiritual term for secrecy) is an important consideration, the meetings should be held at 2:00 A.M. on Tuesdays at a Denny's restaurant at least thirty-five miles away from the church.

③ **Survey the church congregation.**

Everybody has an opinion about what kind of person should be hired as the new pastor. A congregational survey gives everyone an opportunity to express his or her opinion. A lengthy written questionnaire should be designed for this purpose and distributed to every church member. It is very important that the responses be made anonymously. This gives the appearance that the committee encourages candidness. Actually, the purpose for anonymity is so the committee members don't have to lie when someone asks, "Did you read my survey response?"

④ **Develop a job description.**

A preliminary step in every pastor search is the development of a job description. Typically, the job requirements for the new pastor include everything that Jesus Christ did, plus a little bit more.

⑤ **Develop a profile for the perfect candidate.**

Based on the responses to the congregational surveys (if they were read) and the job description, the search committee must then devise a profile of the ideal pastoral candidate. Typically, the profile will end up looking a lot like the drawings of Jesus Christ, although many churches will want their pastor to cut his hair shorter.

⑥ **Investigate all leads.**

It is the responsibility of the committee members to find potential candidates. Since preaching is such an important aspect of the new pastor's job, the committee members must travel considerable distances to hear pastors preaching in their current churches. Based on the expense reimbursement vouchers of the Pastor Search Committee, it will appear that there are many great preachers in Hawaii, Florida, and Aspen, Colorado.

⑦ **Pick a candidate.**

Eventually, the search has to be narrowed down to one candidate. Without a doubt, this will be a fine candidate with many qualities and abilities that God can use to promote spiritual growth in the church. Surprisingly, however, this candidate will bear little resemblance to the "profile" that was developed in Step #5. That is why the committee never disseminates the profile until Step #9.

(8) **Do a sell job on the candidate.**

The person who is selected as the candidate will probably be actively engaged in a successful ministry. This person will have to be persuaded that the present job should be abandoned for an unknown and untested situation at the new church. This is a particularly "hard sell" if the candidate is happy in his current situation and wasn't looking for a job change. In anticipation of this problem, members of the Pastor Search Committee should commit the following phrase to memory: "It seems that it is God's will that you prayerfully consider this ministry opportunity."

(9) **Do a sell job on the congregation.**

Let's assume that the target candidate agrees to be considered for the job. At this point, the word *candidate* becomes a verb as well as a noun (as in "Rev. So-and-So will be candidating at our church next Sunday"). Actually, the Rev. So-and-So and the Pastor Search Committee have agreed that he will be hired. The only obstacle is to make the congregation think that they get to vote on the matter. It is at this point that the Search Committee manipulates the "ideal candidate profile" so it looks exactly like Rev. So-and-So. *Now* the profile can be distributed to the church members.

⑩ **Schedule the candidating sermon.**

Before the congregational vote (see Step #11), the candidate will be required to preach a sermon in the church. It is natural to expect that the candidate will recycle a past sermon that received critical acclaim. However, you must make sure that the candidate actually has more than one good sermon in the arsenal. The Search Committee should bring a halt to the process if the candidate delivers a great Christmas sermon but is preaching on Mother's Day.

⑪ **Take a congregational vote.**

Two things are essential in this step: There actually has to be a vote, and it has to be unanimous. However, every church congregation has a few stubborn dissidents, so the circumstances of the congregational vote have to be carefully strategized. But any irregularity will be suspect. Therefore, we suggest a defensible rationale for the scheduling of the congregational vote: Conduct the vote at the next regularly scheduled meeting of the Pastor Search Committee.

(Now you know the real reason that we suggested Committee meetings at 2:00 A.M. on Tuesdays at a Denny's restaurant at least thirty-five miles away from the church).

Before long, the new pastor will arrive at the church and begin a long and fruitful ministry. Although the church members were apprehensive during the prolonged process, everyone at the church can now sleep soundly (except for the members of the Pastor Search Committee who awake at 2:00 A.M. every Tuesday with a craving for French fries and a turkey club sandwich).

CHAPTER 20

How to Make Sense Out of Your Church Finances

Churches and money have an uncomfortable relationship. A church exists to glorify God, build up believers, and witness to seekers. You will never see "make money" added to the list. However, a church must generate income in order to do the things a church needs to do—such as finance buildings, pay the pastor, support missionaries, and maintain a three-year supply of Hawaiian Punch for church socials. And how does a church do this? Through the generous donations—called "tithes and offerings"—of people like you.

Most people trust their church with the money they give, but they don't always understand where those tithes and offerings go. To help you better understand the intricate and sometimes mysterious world of church finances, here are several things you should know:

1. **There is a difference between tithes and offerings.** When most people hear the word "tithe," they probably think of a ten-percent tax levied by the church. While it's true that the Bible talks about tithes in terms of one-tenth, they are never presented as

mandatory. In Bible times people gave God a tenth of their produce, flocks, and cattle as a way of telling Him "Thanks for blessing us." Offerings were additional gifts to God's work.

Today we still tend to apply that ten-percent rule to tithing so we can support the church at home and missionaries abroad. Offerings are those "over and above" gifts we give for special projects, such as new buildings or year-end budget shortfalls. Most people see their tithe as a "baseline," while an offering is more like a "bonus." That's not a bad way to look at it, as long as we give those bonuses cheerfully.

② **Most people who work on church finances are not professionals.**

Take a look at the photo on the next page. Here's a guy who's working hard to balance the books of his church. His name is Don, and he's the head of the Finance Committee, which means he does this on a volunteer basis. Larger churches can afford to hire a bookkeeper, but your average church must rely on the services of guys like Don.

Don takes his work seriously, as you can see. Even though he's doing this work at home, he feels it's important to dress up as if he were in an office. Don knows that it just wouldn't be right to sort out the

Lord's money wearing jeans and an old sweatshirt.

③ **Churches must be open about their finances.**
Churches aren't like the government or your
employer. They can't hide their finances. Churches
have to be open and report every dollar that comes in
and goes out. There are at least three different ways a
church can share information with its members:

> **The Church Signboard.** This is an old method
> still used in many churches. On a wall at the front

of the sanctuary, an oak signboard displays a few vital statistics: 138 people attended church last week; a total of $98.35 was received in the offering; and the hymn numbers for today's service are 56, 251, and 419. This can be an effective way of communicating important information, as long as people don't start using the numbers to play the lottery.

The Church Bulletin. These days most churches report their weekly or monthly finances in the bulletin (see Chapter 2). Watch for columns labeled "Total Budget," "Received to Date," and "Budget to Date." If the "Received to Date" amount is less than the "Budget to Date" amount, then you haven't been giving your fair share.

The Annual Church Business Meeting. For those who haven't been paying attention to the church signboard or the bulletin throughout the year, this spirited meeting is the best place to catch up on the church's financial picture. The only problem is that the people who speak up and complain that "the pastor is making more than me" don't know a thing about money and haven't dropped anything in the collection plate since last Christmas.

④ **Your pastor is probably underpaid.**

It's true that your pastor is paid more than some of the people in your congregation. These would be your basic deadbeats and unemployed actors. The large majority of the people in your church (this would include anyone earning slightly above the minimum wage) earn more money than your pastor. Considering what the typical pastor has to endure in the course of his career—including, but not limited to, unbearable scrutiny, unwarranted criticism, and constant second-guessing—he or she is woefully underpaid. In fact, if you were to add up the hours your pastor spends preparing sermons, administrating the staff, counseling the hurting, visiting the sick, responding to complaints, and rescuing cats out of trees—then minimum wage would seem like a dream. As it is, the vast majority of pastors do what they do with a firm commitment to God and an unwavering loyalty to their parishioners, regardless of the pay. Just the same, don't you think they should be paid more than your average 7-Eleven employee?

CHAPTER 21

How to Encourage Your Leaders

Church leadership is often a thankless job. Of course, sincere leaders don't do it for the praise or recognition of the congregation. Their service is motivated by a love of God. Nonetheless, an "extra star in their crown" seems rather unfulfilling when they are working hard and getting nothing but grief from the people they are serving.

Your church leaders make a personal sacrifice of time and their own family life for the sake of the church family. They take seriously their sacred calling to spiritually lead, feed, and protect the church congregation. It is in your own best interest to help them in their ministry.

Criticism comes easily, but it usually isn't very productive. If your church leaders aren't pleasing you with their performance, maybe you are partially responsible for their deficiencies. Think about this: Your church leaders can more effectively serve you if you help them rather than hassle them. They can better minister to you if you support them rather than sabotage them.

Make a commitment to God that you will faithfully support and encourage the leaders in your church. Start by praying for them on a regular basis. There is no greater encouragement than that. After you have been praying for them for a while, you'll be surprised at the improvement. . . in their effectiveness and in your attitude toward them.

Obey your spiritual leaders and do what they say.
Their work is to watch over your souls, and they
know they are accountable to God. Give them reason
to do this joyfully and not with sorrow.

HEBREWS 13:17

The best way to encourage
your church leaders is to pray
for them.

CHAPTER 22

How to Memorize Bible Verses

Church is one of the few places where it is still considered a virtue to memorize sections of written text. In the old days (when your parents were in school), teachers required students to memorize historical documents such as the Preamble to the Constitution or the Gettysburg Address. In the really old days (when your grandparents were in school), students had to memorize poetry and recite it perfectly while the teachers towered over them in a menacing fashion, ready to use a wooden ruler to crack the knuckles of any nervous kid who dared miss a word.

These days students aren't asked to memorize prose or poetry (unless you place the Periodic Table of the Elements in either category). And people who are out of school have a hard enough time keeping all of their passwords and PIN numbers straight. Who has time to memorize anything else?

That brings us back to the church. Here is the only place where people still commit passages of written text to memory. Mostly they memorize Bible verses, mainly because they've been told it's a good idea. And where does that idea come from? Well, the Bible for starters. David wrote this psalm: "I have hidden your word in my heart, that I might not sin against you" (Psalm 119:11). The idea is that knowing a few Bible verses "by heart" will help keep you in God's good graces.

In the event that you want to make an attempt to memorize a few key Bible verses, here are three different popular approaches. Depending on your personality type, one of these methods is sure to work for you:

① **The Positive Reinforcement Approach**

This method of memorizing Bible verses works well for people of all ages, but it is especially effective with grade school-age kids. You can try this at home with various kinds of incentives, such as cash or candy, but most kids seem to memorize best when their reward is a little piece of cloth, otherwise known as a merit badge. The Boy and Girl Scouts have used this method for nearly a hundred years with great success. More recently, church-based organizations like Awana and Boys Brigade have been successful in getting kids to memorize vast quantities of Bible verses, passages, and entire chapters, with the simple reward of a patch and the promise of public recognition and possibly a small trophy.

② **The Negative Reinforcement Approach**

This method has fallen out of favor recently, but

there was a time when you could convince a junior high or high school student to memorize Bible verses in order to avoid public humiliation (these days public humiliation is more of a virtue to a junior higher). In the old days (remember them?) ambitious students volunteered to compete in so-called "Sword Drills," based more on exceptional physical reflexes than an uncanny ability to memorize. It wasn't enough to be the first one in a group of contestants to raise your hand when asked to recite "Matthew 6:33" or "Romans 10:9." You had to leap to your feet with lightning speed.

(3) **The Reflective Reinforcement Approach**

While both the positive and negative reinforcement approaches have their place, neither one places the emphasis where it belongs—on the Bible verses themselves. The promise of winning a merit badge or the avoidance of losing a contest offer temporary satisfaction at best. What you want are long-term benefits. That's why we recommend the reflective reinforcement approach to Scripture memory. This method doesn't promise material rewards, and you won't get all worked up into a competitive frenzy. But you will have inner peace and contentment as you reflect on God's Word. Just look at the young man pictured below. He isn't worried about merit badges. He isn't thinking about ways to improve his vertical leap. He's just memorizing a Bible verse. Either that, or he's wondering why he's the only one in his peer group who still wears argyle socks.

CHAPTER 23

How to Get a Perfect Attendance Pin

Sunday school has everything that a young child desires: crackers, juice, toys, and crafts. As the toddler gets a little older, however, the motivation needs to be cranked up a notch. Beginning at the kindergarten stage, some churches implement the reward system of the "perfect attendance" pin. If the child attends the entire year without missing a Sunday, then he or she is awarded with a decorative badge to acknowledge the feat of perfect attendance.

But it doesn't stop there. For each successive year of perfect attendance, the pin grows larger. Finally, when the pin is about the size of a saucer, further accolades take the form of bars that hang from the pin. If the kid makes it all the way through high school with perfect attendance, he or she is then sporting a chest full of hardware.

Perfect attendance doesn't come easy. It takes the cooperative efforts of the entire family. Together, as a fighting unit, they must employ several shrewd strategies:

① **Infirmity is no impediment.**
   You can't let a little illness stand in the way of victory. No matter how sick your kid is, an hour of Sunday school won't be fatal.

② **Disease is no deterrent.**

It doesn't matter that your child may infect the other kids with mumps, measles, or meningitis. In the high stakes game of attendance-pin poker, the weak deserve to be weeded out.

Winston is thirty-seven years old and hasn't missed a Sunday since before kindergarten. He was disappointed to learn that the attendance pin awards don't extend beyond high school, but he found another way to bring attention to his accomplishment of perfect attendance.

③ **Double your chances.**

Parents of identical twins can double their chances for success. However, plans must be implemented before the first Sunday of the kindergarten year. Register only one child. Do not disclose the fact that you have twins. Hold one child in "reserve" in the event that the enrolled child rebels during the tumultuous teenage years and skips church for the lure of Starbucks.

④ **Don't ignore the inside job.**

Develop your computer skills so you can hack into the church's computer system and alter the attendance records if your child misses a Sunday or two. Be prepared to join some ministry of the church that entitles you to carry a "master key" to the church office.

⑤ **If all else fails, teach.**

You may need to volunteer to be the teacher of the kindergarten Sunday school class to ensure that your child's initial records are exemplary (even if his or her actual attendance is spotty). Of course, you may need to prolong your Sunday school teaching ruse for another twelve years, moving up a grade on an annual basis to protect the perfection of your progeny's phony presence.

If you are a realist, you have already calculated that thirteen years of perfect attendance requires 676 Sundays without a miss. It will be a lot easier if you simply try to find a complete set of perfect attendance pins at a garage sale. These treasures are hard to find, so you might have to get up early on a Saturday morning and go to every garage sale and swap meet in your area. But if you find one, you can celebrate by sleeping in the next day and skipping church.

CHAPTER 24

How to Tell the Difference Between Catechism, Confirmation, Communion, and Confession

One of the more mysterious and sometimes confusing aspects of the church is Bible doctrine. The very word *doctrine* sounds so technical and rigid, like some kind of medical device that's going to hurt a whole lot. Actually, doctrine simply refers to the beliefs and principles presented in the Bible, which means that it's filled with all kinds of complicated concepts and words you never hear outside of the church (see Chapter 6).

It's hard enough for adults to grasp the basics of church and Bible doctrine, yet most churches have developed a system of classroom instruction in order to teach these complex issues to the youngsters, usually starting with fifth and sixth graders. This instruction has different names, depending on the type of church you attend. If you go to a Catholic church, you are likely to take *catechism* classes. Protestants generally call the whole process confirmation. And then there's communion and confession, which are different, yet somehow related to catechism and confirmation. If you're totally confused (something that is perfectly natural), here is a guideline to these basic terms and their meanings:

① **Catechism**

Technically, *catechism* is a manual of doctrine written in the form of questions and answers, but the term has come to include the entire process of learning basic Bible doctrine. The Catholics were the first to use a book and classroom instruction to teach people the basics of the faith. If you went to church as a kid, catechism was mandatory (at least that's what your parents told you). Most kids learned a great deal, not because the material was so interesting, but because the classes were taught by rather menacing-looking (to a kid) priests and nuns who said you would come to no good if you didn't memorize everything down to the smallest detail.

② **Confirmation**

Protestants have the same type of instruction, but they call it *confirmation.* And instead of having professionals teach the doctrine, your average Baptist or Methodist churches leave it to average people (the church calls them *lay-men*, even when women are involved) to teach impressionable youngsters basic Bible doctrine and church history. Notice the photo of Mrs. Crump's confirmation class, which includes bonus piano lessons. The conservative attire worn by these girls tells you that this is a Baptist confirmation class (Methodist girls would be wearing much more "worldly" outfits).

③ **Communion**

In some church circles, *communion* is like a dedication for infants, as in First Communion. This ceremony usually involves baptism, lacy clothing, and tiny white Bibles. In most churches communion describes the ceremony of remembrance involving grape juice (or wine if you're in a Catholic church) and bread (or wafers), symbolizing the sacrifice of Christ's body for the church. Completion of catechism or confirmation is usually a prerequisite for taking communion, although you won't find the minister or priest asking for a certificate before administering the "elements."

④ **Confession**

This word covers a variety of activities. In a personal and private sense, *confession* means admitting wrong-doing and then asking God's forgiveness for your sins. But confession can also mean a public declaration of the basic doctrines you learn in catechism or confirmation. The Westminster Confession of Faith and the Apostles' Creed are the most famous confessions. In some churches (although this is becoming a lost art), the congregation collectively recites the Confession or Creed in the same way you might recite the Lord's Prayer.

If you went to church as a youngster, you may remember being involved in all or some of these rather formal activities. Regardless of your church involvement today, you probably still remember some of the things you learned and did when you were a kid. That's the good thing about catechism, confirmation, communion, and confession. Learning about God and the Bible, remembering what Jesus did on the cross, and confessing to God what we know to be true always has value, regardless of your age.

CHAPTER 25

How to Make a Replica of the Sistine Chapel
(Using Only Pipe Cleaners and a Lanyard)

If you read the title of this chapter and actually believed it, then you have the requisite optimism and are sufficiently detached from reality to fulfill the church's most prestigious position: Children's Crafts Coordinator.

The importance of children's crafts cannot be overestimated:

① **Crafts keep the kids occupied in "children's church."** This is particularly important when the pastor's sermon is like a car on the freeway that passes a lot of exits but never takes the off-ramp.

② **Crafts keep the kids occupied during summer camp.** Sports are an outdoor activity, but the craft table can be placed indoors. Most adults know this. So does the camp director. That why the director wants to advertise the fact that you will be in charge of crafts. Sign-ups for adult counselors go quickly if they have a chance to work in an air-conditioned room with sedate little artisans instead of standing in one hundred-plus degree weather with yelling, sweaty, pint-sized athletes.

③ **Crafts are a profit center for the church.**
The children's department is usually the only profit-making ministry in the church. It is all about low overhead and high profit margin. The kids make cotton ball sculptures and construction paper mobiles and get paid nothing for their effort (thanks to the church's exemption from child labor laws). These items are then sold at the church bazaar for exorbitant prices to the parents of the little artists. It's a scam, but no mother or father has the gumption to buck the system and risk being labeled a bad parent.

If you assume the position of children's craft coordinator, you will need to clear your garage of all tools, bicycles, and vehicles. The entirety of your garage must be reserved for your "craft supplies." (A basement can also be used for this purpose, but the frequent trips up and down the stairs while you are carrying a fifty-gallon drum of rubber cement can present a safety hazard.)

Your job as children's craft coordinator will also involve a limited amount of public speaking. At least once a month, you will be giving an announcement in church, asking the membership to collect the components for your next project. The most frequently requested items will be:

- used milk cartons (half-gallon size);
- cottage cheese containers (twenty-four-ouncesize);
- egg cartons (one dozen size);
- shoe boxes; and
- unopened cans of Hershey's chocolate syrup.

Actually, you won't need chocolate syrup for any craft. The stash of Hershey's chocolate syrup in your kitchen cupboard will be your reward for spending the Saturday night before Christmas cutting out 137 nativity scenes, complete with camels, wise men, and the baby Jesus.

CHAPTER 26

How to Make a Shepherd's Costume Out of a Bathrobe

The most exciting time of the entire year for churches everywhere is Christmas. This is the time when we celebrate the birth of Jesus, who is the reason for the season and the foundation of the church itself. Knowing that more people will stream through the church during the Christmas season than any other time of year, the pastor puts in overtime developing the best sermons possible. The music department gears up for the Christmas "cantata," while the church drama director spends months preparing for the Christmas "pageant," typically a period piece set in Bible times—complete with a manger, a backdrop of the little town of Bethlehem, and maybe even a live sheep or goat.

When it comes to putting together a cast, the pageant director must first find the perfect Mary and Joseph and baby Jesus (usually played by a life-sized doll). The part of Mary is fairly demanding, because she needs to know how to recite the "Magnificat," or at least have the ability to show the audience that she is pondering things in her heart. By contrast, Joseph just needs to stand by Mary's side and appear supportive.

An adventurous pageant director will cast the part of an angel to represent the "heavenly host," complete with rudimentary riggings to simulate the appearance of flight. The parts of the three wise men (also known as the Magi) are coveted roles, mostly because they get to dress up in glittery costumes and carry ornate boxes filled with "gold, frankincense, and myrrh." Then there are the shepherds. Since these are non-speaking characters (all they have to do is look terrified as they hold their hands in front of their faces to shield them from the blinding angelic light), pageant directors like to assign these roles to the boys with a reputation for rowdiness. That way, if they act up during the pageant, there's no harm done. Audiences will think that's what shepherds naturally do.

This overall shepherd's demeanor is reflected in their clothing. There's no glitter or glamour here, just loose-fitting tunics. Over the years pageant directors have found that the shepherd's garb is the easiest to create, mainly because every household already has the basic costume every church pageant shepherd wears: the everyday bathrobe.

In the event that you or a member of your family should ever be called upon to play a shepherd in the church Christmas pageant, here are some tips for turning a bathrobe into an authentic period costume:

An old flannel robe works best. This is the kind of robe your father or your grandfather used to wear. Ideally it should look like someone has been sleeping in it for ten years, which is exactly what the shepherds did in their clothing.

Besides looking like they belong on shepherds, bathrobes are practical for another very important reason. Because there's so much extra material, they can be overlapped in front like a double-breasted suit and tied securely, thereby avoiding any possibility that the robe will come undone, revealing shorts, rolled-up jeans, or a T-shirt with characters from *South Park* emblazoned on the front.

When securing the robe, it's more authentic to use a length of frayed rope rather than a leather belt. In an emergency, it's acceptable to borrow a velvet pew rope from the church, although this is probably a little fancy for a shepherd and more befitting of a wise man's costume.

If you can't find a flannel robe, a robe made from terry cloth will do, although it should not be too white or fluffy or have the words "Greenbrier Resort & Spa" embroidered on the front pocket, making you look like you just came from the health club rather than the fields tending your flocks by night.

To look even more authentic, make sure the shepherds stand between other pageant participants dressed in "civilian" clothing, such as is shown in the picture. These  would be the narrators, chosen for their roles on the basis of failing to come up with suitable bathrobes of their own.

No matter how hard the entire cast rehearses, it's important to remember that inevitably something will go wrong: Someone will forget their lines, a piece of scenery will begin to peel away, or the live goat will decide to, well, be a goat. Don't worry—the audience won't mind. In fact, that's one of the reasons people come to Christmas pageants in the first place. Yes, they want to be reminded of the greatest night in history, but they also take comfort in the fact that the plaid bathrobes on the shepherds remind them of their grandpas.

CHAPTER 27

How to Properly Videotape the Christmas Program

A child's performance in the church Christmas program is a rite of passage. It involves nervous jitters, upset stomachs, sweaty palms, and migraine headaches. The kids don't suffer from these symptoms. These are the agonies of any parent who has the responsibility to videotape a child's performance.

The conditions for videotaping the Christmas program are always less than ideal. You'll be in fierce competition with the other parents for the best filming location. This is no place for video rookies.

① Preproduction

Attend several of the dress rehearsals so you can plan for the best camera angle. Forget about centering the shot for the entire group. Make a mental note of where your kid will be standing and plan for a camera angle that features your child.

② Set Up

Arrive early to stake the claim to your preplanned seat. We suggest making a special trip to the church in the morning and placing a sign on your selected chair that reads: "Reserved for the Pastor."

③ **Set Design**

Church platforms are designed for a pastor to be seen above the heads of the congregation. Your child is probably shorter than the pastor, so the platform might not be high enough to make your child visible. Have your child stand on a stack of hymnals, if necessary.

④ **Lighting**

You might need to bring in extra lighting to illuminate the stage brighter than usual. Typical church lighting is diffused in order to avoid glare off the heads of the bald men in the choir loft.

⑤ **Blocking**

"Blocking" is a theatrical term that refers to the planned movement by actors across the stage. In your case, *blocking* refers to some other kid getting in your camera shot. Make sure your child knows that nothing or no one should get between his or her face and your camera lens. If time allows, teach your child a few basic karate moves that can be employed to protect his or her "space" on stage.

⑥ Sound

Church sound systems are unreliable. To make matters worse, video camera microphones are omnidirectional and will pick up the whirl of the myriad other video cameras being used by all of the other parents. We suggest that you purchase a wireless lapel microphone attachment for your camera. Strap the microphone and transmitter to your child prior to the performance. This equipment is a little pricey, but you can pay for it

Don't let the expanse of the sanctuary fool you. You don't need a wide-angle lens on your video camera. Stick with the telephoto lens. Capturing the other children on your video isn't important. Your kid is the only one who matters. Zoom in with a tight, close-up on your kid and stay that way.

from the money you would otherwise put in the Christmas offering. (After all, it is the church's fault that you have to buy the wireless mike in the first place. If the church had a better sound system, you wouldn't be forced to buy this extra equipment.)

(7) **Postproduction**

This step is the most important of all. After your tape has been made, put a label on it, and punch out those tabs on the cassette (the ones that prevent you from recording over the tape again). There is nothing more tragic than sitting down to watch the video of the church's Christmas program with your child only to see that you accidentally recorded over the tape with a rerun of *It's a Very Brady Christmas*.

CHAPTER 28

How to Work in the Nursery
(Without Losing Your Mind)

Everybody who goes to church is a volunteer participant. Even though you will sometimes hear military terms in the church service (such as the hymn "Onward, Christian Soldiers"), there's no such thing as a "draft" that conscripts people into the "Lord's Army." (The only exception to this might be a reluctant kid or a recalcitrant husband—or is it the other way around?—who tries to avoid church at all costs but who gets drafted into going to church by a strong-willed mother/wife.)

Once you get into the routine of willingly going to church, you still don't *have* to do anything. You can just sit there, or you can voluntarily choose to participate in a variety of activities: singing in the choir, teaching Sunday school, ushering, etc. Even the offering is voluntary.

Having said that, it must be pointed out that there is one area in the church where the workers aren't volunteers at all, and that's the nursery. Truth be told, nursery workers have been drafted into service. Oh, they may tell you that they are delighted to take care of other people's screaming, squirming, squirting infants, but don't be fooled. Nursery workers are doing their jobs under extreme duress. Just in case you have not yet been drafted to work in the nursery, here are some categories of people who are prime candidates for nursery duty:

You are a dad who once had a baby of his own in the nursery.

Your baby's name was Michael, but he was known by the nursery workers as Stinky (for obvious reasons) or Banshee, mainly because he screamed from the minute you dropped him off until you picked him up again two hours later. Now that your kid has graduated from the nursery to the toddler room, you feel obligated to serve your "time" so you can make up for all the grief your little Michael caused.

You are a mom who is planning to have a baby in the next year.

You know how the system works. You are fully aware that if your new little angel is to get the royal treatment from the nursery workers, you are going to have to become a nursery worker yourself, so you decide to get your service out of the way before your little one arrives.

You are a candidate for grandmotherhood, but you don't have any grandchildren.

All of your subtle hints to your kids and their spouses have fallen on deaf ears. Your kids are married and yet they haven't seen fit to produce the one thing you have to look forward to in your twilight years: grandchildren of your own. So you grudgingly work in the church nursery, but you tell your kids that it's the most wonderful experience in the world. You tell them that you have never been happier, although it still isn't like having grandchildren of your own.

You are a teenager who wants to serve God in an "extreme" way.

You signed up for the summer trip to Outer Mongolia, but you weren't able to raise enough money to go, so you figure that the nursery is the next most extreme church experience you can have. In order to enhance your three-month stint, you wear clothing from the Travelsmith catalog and smuggle Bibles into the cribs.

Even if you don't fall into one of these categories, chances are that you will be drafted into the nursery at some point in your church experience, even if it's only for a few months. When that happens, you will be grateful to know these survival tips:

1. Do not be alarmed when various liquids, airborne droplets, and semisolid matter flow from a baby's body. This is very normal. To avoid direct contact with these substances, wear a smock or a colorful serape, a pair of sterile gloves, and a surgeon's mask.

2. Be prepared to endure shrieking sounds that register in the decibel range of a jet engine. And that's just the noise coming from your fellow workers! To protect yourself from screaming babies, wear a pair of earplugs, preferably ones approved for arena rock concerts.

③ Become familiar with the nursery numbering system. In most church nurseries each infant is issued a number so that a parent can be contacted should an emergency arise. Usually an announcement like this is made over the church intercom system: "Will the owner of Baby #911 please come to the nursery? Your baby is holding one of our workers hostage."

④ To add variety to your nursery routine, try altering your appearance each time you work. Wear a clever costume, put on the mask of a *Sesame Street* character, or simply talk in a funny voice. This may distract the babies and prevent them from engaging in their usual antics. Another benefit is that the parents won't know who to blame when they find out that you improperly changed all the diapers.

⑤ Finally, don't be surprised when, at the end of your nursery service, you sign up for another tour of duty. Sometimes those precious little ones have a way of getting to you (and we mean that in a good way).

CHAPTER 29

How to Grow a Kid

Sometimes little children in the congregation are referred to as "the future of the church." References of this sort minimize the importance and value of the children at their present age. Children are no less a part of the church just because they are young. Maybe they can't vote at a congregational meeting, and maybe they need a boost at the drinking fountain, but they are definitely an integral part of the church family right now.

Jesus had a special fondness for children. Scripture doesn't record Christ ever saying: "Suffer the thirties and forties to come unto me." No, it was the children that He invited to sit with Him. In the same way, every church family should value the importance of their children.

Statistics reveal that the majority of adult church members made a commitment to God as children. This means that children's ministries in the church are much more than just a child-care convenience for the parents. The time that a child spends at the church is really an opportunity to teach that child about God. Adults who work in the children's ministries are not baby-sitters; with every word and loving gesture, they teach those little kids about the heavenly Father.

When you see someone working in the nursery or teaching a children's class at church, thank them for their ministry. Better yet, pray for them. Even better, join in their ministry. God wants to show His love to those children, and He may want to do it through you.

> *Teach your children to choose the right path, and*
> *when they are older, they will remain upon it.*
>
> PROVERBS 22:6

CHAPTER 30

How to Survive Junior High Church

Ask anybody who's ever been in junior high, who is the parent of a junior higher, who teaches junior high kids, or who is now a junior high school student: What's it like? And they will answer: Huh? Or they may look at you with a blank stare and then suddenly run in the opposite direction.

This is because anyone even remotely connected with a junior high person is not currently in his or her right mind. They may look normal, but in fact they are temporarily insane. We stress the word *temporarily,* because the good news about the junior high experience is that it lasts only two years. But those two years make walking through a minefield look like a stroll in the park.

It's hard enough being a Monday–Friday junior higher in regular school. Your body is going through all of these changes, your emotions are bouncing around like a video game gone bad, and to top it off, you have to learn algebra (which in itself is enough to drive anybody crazy).

Then comes Sunday and you have to play the game all over again with an entirely different group of people, your junior high youth group at church. Isn't that just adding more fuel to the junior high fire? How do you survive junior high church?

Here are some tips you may want to pass on to a junior high young person near you. The life you save may just be your own (or your own kid's):

① **Understand that junior high kids are maturing at different rates.**

At no time in the life of a human being do people who are about the same age look so different. Because of the aforementioned physical changes that happen to all junior highers, it's quite natural for full-grown women to be mixed in with prepubescent boys. To illustrate, on the following page is a picture of a typical junior high church youth group. You will notice three things about the kids in this photo:

- Some kids look older than others.

- Most girls mature faster than most boys.

- Girls in a junior high youth group outnumber boys.

Do not be alarmed. This is the way it is in junior high.

② **Junior high is not the time to make bold fashion statements.**

Notice in the photo the tall girl in the back row

wearing the polka-dot dress. She clearly stands out from the crowd. Notice how uncomfortable she looks. This is because she is the only one wearing polka dots. Junior high is the time to blend in, not stand out.

③ **Don't worry that junior high kids are not mentioned in the Bible.**

The Bible has lots to say about children:

- *Children* are a gift from the Lord; they are a reward from him.

- Her *children* stand and bless her.

- Jesus said, "Let the *children* come to me. Don't stop them!"

You will notice that the Bible doesn't say, "*Junior highers* are a gift from God." If a *junior high* young person ever told his mom, "You're the best," she would probably faint. If Jesus had said, "Let the *junior high* kids come to Me," His disciples would have run for cover.

And what about that child who brought the loaves and fishes to Jesus so He could multiply them and feed the five thousand hungry people on the hillside? If he had been in junior high, the young man would probably have brought Jesus frogs from his science class and the rubber soles of his worn-out Nikes.

Even Jesus the junior higher isn't mentioned in Scripture. The last we read about Jesus as a child is when He was twelve years old. The Bible skips His junior high years altogether.

There's a reason for these deliberate omissions. Even though the junior high years are perfectly natural, there's no reason we have to put our experiences in writing. Some things are better left unsaid and unwritten.

④ **Recognize that junior high lasts only two years— three years, tops.**

This is the best news of all when it comes to being in junior high or relating to someone who is. You can survive anything for two years, as long you know there is a normal and productive life waiting on the other side.

CHAPTER 31

How to Be Cool in High School

Whether they will admit it or not, teenagers want to be *cool*. This is a universal struggle that confronts all young people, but there are unique challenges for teenagers in the church-case scenario.

The characteristics that contribute to a kid's "cool quotient" cannot be quantitatively described. In fact, any cool teenager will tell you that if you don't know what cool is, you definitely don't have it. That very statement exhibits the essence of what cool is all about: attitude. Oh, sure, cool also involves aspects of fashion, body posture, and linguistics, but those factors are all influenced by an overriding attitude. If the kid has a cool attitude, then everything he or she does, wears, or says will be cool.

At its core, the attitude of cool is all about rebellion. The cool kids at the high school seem to have a disdain, or at least a disinterest, toward authority and traditional family values. And therein lies the conundrum for the teenager in the church youth group. The church kids will definitely lose all hope of being considered cool if their tattoos say things like:

- Honor Your Mother and Father;
- Submit to Those in Authority Over You;
- Lips That Touch Liquor Will Never Touch Mine;
- I Don't Smoke and I Don't Chew, and I Won't Date the Ones Who Do; or
- The Only People I Will Date: Those Who Are Fit to Be My Marriage Mate.

Thus, for the church teenager, cool must be defined by a different paradigm. The *attitude* of cool must be abandoned because it violates biblical principles. In its place, church teenagers must substitute and rely heavily on outward appearances. They can look rebellious on the outside, but they can be sweet and religious on the inside. This works out perfectly because, as the Scripture says, people look at the outward appearance but God looks on the heart.

Here are the ways that church kids can look cool:

Change clothes immediately after church. As a general rule, the apparel that is acceptable for teenagers to wear at church is not cool in the outside world. Therefore, teenagers should not go directly from church to the mall. There must be an intervening costume change. (Note: This rule does not apply to teenagers who go to one of those mega-churches that is already in the shopping mall.)

Each outfit should make the parents cringe.
Parents may flatly prohibit a teenager from wearing styles that are too offensive or revealing. Consequently, the teenager cannot go overboard. The choice of clothing should be something that will stretch the boundary of the parental dress code without shattering it. Here is the goal: The teenager wants to hear a complaint or a sarcastic criticism from the parent while still being allowed to exit the house. If there is *no* complaint or criticism, then the teenager should change clothes immediately. Any apparel that a parent actually approves of is definitely not cool.

Don't forget to accessorize. Once the teenager has gone a safe distance from church or home, temporary accessories can be added to make his or her ensemble complete. A fake tattoo can be achieved with a few artistic strokes of a Sharpie pen. A pocket-sized New Testament can be rolled in a shirtsleeve or tucked into a hip pocket to give the illusion of a pack of cigarettes. An office stapler can be used for a quick body piercing.

You are what you drive. All attempts at appearing cool will be futile unless the teenager is seen in the proper car. For a church kid, the mode of a teenager's transportation is the greatest factor in determining coolness.

The assessment is made on a car-by-car basis, but there are a few generally accepted principles.

The car may be cool if it has any of the following features:

- a big engine;

- a convertible top; or

- a stereo system that can rattle the rib cage of pedestrians within a three-block radius.

Biff (his real name is Francis) knows that being cool at church is all about how you look and the car you drive. Although not visible in this photograph, he keeps his trophy for Bible verse memorization in the trunk of the car.

The car will definitely *not* be cool if it has any of the following features:

- a church bulletin on the dashboard;

- a box of Pampers in the back seat that needs to be delivered to the church nursery; or

- a radio tuned into grandma's favorite religious station that only plays hymns sung by male quartets accompanied by a pipe organ.

A kid's cool quotient will also be impacted by his or her peer group. In other words, does the kid hang out with other cool kids? Here again, the church teenager is put into an awkward position. There are always a few kids in the youth group who have no clue or concept about being cool. These noncool church kids are easily identified within the youth group. They are the ones who say things like "I've got a great idea for witnessing to our friends at school. Let's invite them to the Gospel Heirs concert this next Saturday night at the Rescue Mission. They are a male quartet that sings hymns, accompanied by a pipe organ. My grandma says that the Gospel Heirs are her favorite group. Grandma says that she'll drive us to the concert in her Buick."

There is not much that the cool church kids can do with the noncool youth group members. That "love one another" verse prohibits public humiliation and derision. Consequently, the Gospel Heirs concert becomes an official youth group "activity." Even the cool kids from the church will end up going when they realize that standing on the street corner in the bad part of town after the concert will make them look rebellious.

CHAPTER 32

How to Put on a Successful Youth Banquet

Like the hula hoop and the Pet Rock, the church youth banquet has pretty much faded from the cultural scene. However, there was a time when high school youth groups everywhere put on their own version of the high school prom, only without the dancing. The youth sponsors and student leaders would form a banquet committee and plan months in advance for an event that would rival anything the high schools could come up with (only without the dancing).

Some of the guys in the youth group would ask some of the girls in the youth group to be their "dates," while others would bring dates from other churches, or sometimes from no church at all (the kids who did this considered it "outreach"). Everybody always wondered what kind of "worldly" dates would show up.

A bunch of the parents would get together and cook the food, usually spaghetti or some sort of casserole dish. The students would decorate the church Fellowship Hall to create a nonchurchy "mood" (basically this meant hanging some crepe paper streamers and using candles on the church banquet tables rather than relying on the bright and noisy overhead fluorescent lighting). There wouldn't be a band, but the kids would bring their favorite Christian music (something with a beat but not too outrageous), and someone would line up a speaker, usually a bald middle-aged guy with glasses who was hip to the youth "lingo."

The banquet was usually a lot of fun—if uneventful—leaving the attendees relatively satisfied, but wondering what it was like to go to the high school prom (where people actually danced).

All of that may seem like a world away, and by all measurements it is. These days churches don't even attempt to put on banquets for their students. That's because things have changed significantly. For one thing, dancing is no longer a taboo for church young people. That's not to say that churches are sponsoring dances (unless it happens spontaneously during a service in some charismatic churches as an "outpouring of the Spirit"), but they no longer frown upon kids going to their high school proms and formals.

The other factor leading to the demise of the church youth banquet is that high school kids seem to have a lot more money these days. One of the reasons the church youth banquet was so popular was that tickets generally cost no more than five dollars a person, which was an attractive economical alternative to the forty dollar prom "bid." And there were no extra costs involved. You could wear your Sunday suit or your Easter dress and be right in style. Today the kids have no trouble coming up with the cash for a $100 tux, a $150 prom dress, dinner at a fancy restaurant, a $100 prom ticket, and a stretch limo to take five or six couples around town in style.

Knowing they can't compete with the whole high school prom and formal scene, church youth groups these days have become much more creative when it comes to hosting youth events. Here are three popular scenarios:

① **The Missions Banquet**

High school kids love short-term mission projects, where they go to places like Mexico, Haiti, Zimbabwe, or Russia during Easter break or for the entire summer. If a bunch of kids are going, the church will often sponsor a missions banquet. Here is where the kids prepare the spaghetti dinner for the parents and other supportive adults in order to raise money for the trips. There's still no dancing involved.

② **The Twenty-Four-Hour Fast**

Kids today are much more aware of the desperate needs of people around the world. One popular youth event has nothing to do with food, and yet it is all about food. In order to identify with people who have much less than they do (especially food), high school kids will gather in a room at church and fast for twenty-four hours, using the time to pray and learn more about what they can do. Of course, after the twenty-four hours are up, all the starving church kids gorge themselves on fast food at the local hangout.

③ **The Sunday Morning Tux and Formal Fashion Show**
You see this more and more. The way some high school kids figure it, if they're going to go to a Saturday night prom or formal and spend all that money for a tux and a dress, they might as well get their money's worth. So they show up at church the next morning wearing their extravagant outfits, only with the added feature of wrinkles, sweat stains, and food residue. And that's just on the girls. The guys look a whole lot worse.

In days gone by, the youth banquet was an economical alternative to the more expensive high school proms and formals, especially if all you had for dinner was a napkin.

CHAPTER 33

How to Audition for a Church Youth Band

Ever since King David played his harp and lyre and danced before the Lord, people have been anxious to express their musical talents in the church (only without the dancing). For centuries a cappella choral music was all that the church allowed. Then came organ and piano accompaniment, but only if played in a "reverent" style. Finally, in the second half of the twentieth century, the youth movement hit the church, and along with it, the incorporation of the guitar and other stringed instruments (including, but not limited to, the banjo, the ukulele, the upright stringed bass, and the gutbucket).

At first these radical instruments and the disgusting Beatle haircuts that went with them were banished from the sacred confines of the church sanctuary, giving birth to the church youth band. Usually these makeshift folk ensembles were comprised of eager young musicians who had just enough talent to keep from embarrassing themselves and the audience. What they lacked in musical ability, however, they made up for in clean-scrubbed enthusiasm and clever names taken from the nomenclature of the popular "secular" groups and bands that played on the Top 40 AM radio stations.

- "Bought 'n Paid For" was a tribute to the "New Christy Minstrels."
- "The Four Fifths" came from "The Four Freshmen."
- "Lasting Faith" was from the group "Blind Faith."

Merely having a modicum of talent, a clever name, and matching outfits didn't mean that your band could automatically play in front of the youth group on Sunday mornings and Wednesday nights. The church leadership had to audition and approve your band in order to be sure that you didn't incorporate any of the "devil's music" (that would be music with a rock 'n roll beat) into your songs and choruses.

Even though the times have changed (no one plays the gutbucket any more), and the musical styles of today's youth bands have caught up to the current musical styles, the methods used to audition aspiring church youth bands—now called worship bands—have not. In the event that you will ever be asked to audition a band for your church, here are some things to look for:

① **Appearance counts.**

In days gone by, everyone in the band had to have matching outfits and compatible haircuts, such as the young men pictured in the photo on the next page.

Today this is an undesirable look. If a prospective worship band shows up looking like these guys, you should excuse them immediately and refer them to the "Up With People" tryouts.

② **Musical ability is important.**

It used to take more talent to pass a youth band audition, mainly because the instruments were "unplugged." Today's worship bands use so much amplification and reverb that it's difficult to tell which one or two members of the group actually have talent. That's why musical ability is important, but not as important as facial expressions.

③ **Watch the facial expressions.**

Youth bands in years gone by wore happy expressions and made eye contact with the audience. Today this is considered unspiritual for a true worship band. You are looking for a different type of facial expression. The group you are auditioning should never make eye contact, but rather should look upward, or keep their eyes closed altogether. The lead singers should look like they are in their own world, rather than yours.

④ **The banter should overpower the music.**

By *banter* we mean the way the group talks between songs. The ratio of music to banter used to be nine to one or eight to two, at the most. The purpose of talking between songs was to transition from one song to the next. Today it's the other way around. Accomplished worship band leaders will talk twice as much as they sing. In other words, the songs are used to set up the banter.

⑤ **Repetition is desirable.**

Church youth songs used to be one-and-a-half to two minutes long, mainly because the lyrics were limited. (Example: *Kumba yah, my Lord, Kumba yah. . . .*

That's the whole song.) Today, worship chorus lyrics aren't any more involved, but the worship bands repeat them over and over again until the entire audience has either become entranced with the worship experience or gone home for lunch.

There you have it—ome useful guidelines for auditioning youth and worship bands. Remember, times change and people change, but the songs stay the same. No, wait, that can't be right. Times change and the songs change, but people stay the same. No, that doesn't sound right, either. The songs and people stay the same, but the times they are a changin'. Oh, we give up. You get the idea.

CHAPTER 34

How to Properly Maintain the Church Bus

As soon as there are too many kids in the youth group to fit into two minivans, the youth pastor is going to ask the church trustees to acquire a bus for the youth group. The initial request will be denied because the trustees will say that there is "no room in the budget" for the purchase of a church bus. Undaunted, the youth pastor will manage to find a used bus that the church can obtain for free. Typically, this means that the bus will come from the rusting fleet of stunt vehicles used in the filming of *The Partridge Family* television show. And it won't be exactly free. There will be the expense of the tow truck that hauled the bus from the wrecking yard to the church parking lot.

In their enthusiasm, youth pastors only think about the initial purchase price and forget about the expense of maintenance. But trustees don't forget about such things. Trustees have been through this before (with the former youth pastor, who was encouraged to "resign" after the unfortunate fiasco following his plans for a citywide evangelistic campaign that involved every kid in the youth group on a hang glider). Trustees know that the maintenance of a church bus is an expensive undertaking because it must be maintained according to the following standards:

1. **Parental satisfaction.** The parents of the kids in the youth group only care about one thing: Is the bus safe? This consideration involves three elements:

   Is the engine reliable? Parents don't want any mechanical problems at 2:00 A.M. when the youth group is returning from the Spring Break ministry in Mexico. Parents want the bus to be reliable because they don't want to make the drive to Tijuana to pick up a carload of high school kids who haven't showered for a week.)

   Are the tires and brakes in good condition? No kid gets hurt if the bus can't start, but every kid gets hurt if the bus can't stop.

   Will every kid be strapped to his or her seat in a full safety harness? This is a concern for every father of a girl in the youth group. Those dads want to make sure that the boys in the bus are strapped down tight.

2. **Approval by the seniors.** This criterion does not refer to those students who are in their fourth year of high school. We're talking about the senior citizens of

the church. The high school kids refer to them as "the old people" in the church, but they are usually identified as "the seniors." Sometimes the seniors are the most active group in the church. (They may be the only group that has both the time and the money to go places.) If the church acquires a bus, then you can be sure that the seniors will form a travel club and plan lots of trips in the bus. (They'll have a contest to pick a snazzy name for their travel group. It will always end up being the "Wayfarers.") Since the senior constituency is responsible for the largest portion of the offering (and the high voting turnout at the church board elections), the trustees must make sure that the bus is equipped to the satisfaction of the seniors. This means that three features must be present:

An effective public address system. The seniors need to hear the tour guide's voice above the roar of the bus engine. The frequency of the microphone must be calibrated so as not to create static or a high-pitched squeal in hearing aids.

A high-volume heater. An air conditioner is not essential. It will never be used on Wayfarer trips. But the heater is indispensable. These people are always cold.

A bathroom in the rear of the bus. **Wayfarer** groups always make a "rest stop" every thirty miles. But a bathroom on the bus is required just in case someone can't wait that long.

③ **Youth group endorsement.** There is no sense getting a church bus if the kids in the youth group complain about riding in it. But it doesn't take much to keep them happy. The only expenditure necessary for them is the installation and maintenance of video monitors. (Their hopes of watching an R-rated movie on the way to summer camp will be shattered when the youth group sponsor pops in a Focus on the Family video about submission to parental authority.)

Even if the costs of these maintenance expenses can be covered by the church budget, there is an additional problem that the trustees must deal with if the church is considering a bus for the youth group. This is a logistical problem, not a financial one. The church must find someone who is qualified to drive the bus. The youth pastor will volunteer to get a bus driver's license, but the parents will insist that he be prohibited from driving the bus. They have seen how he drives his car, and they don't want to have a parental prayer meeting every time the youth group takes the bus off the church lot.

How to Invite a Friend to Church

It is a common occurrence in churches everywhere. The kids in the youth group are challenged by the pastor to invite a friend to church. This is not an easy task for most church teenagers because they have a preconceived notion that their nonchurch friends will have an aversion to church. Church is okay for the kids in the youth group, but they can't imagine that the idea of "going to church" will appeal to their friends.

To make the invitation process a little easier, the pastor and leaders of the high school group sponsor some type of "youth event" that doesn't seem so churchy. This event typically takes the form of an evangelistic youth concert. It is even booked at the outdoor amphitheater in the park (so the unsuspecting friends won't be immediately tipped off that this is a church event). With this ruse, the kids in the youth group don't invite their friends to *church*; they can invite their friends to a *concert*. But no self-respecting church kid is going to trick his or her nonchurch friends into attending a concert where the highlight is an "invitation to come forward" instead of the performer jumping into the mosh pit. So the church kids have the same dilemma: how to invite a nonchurch friend to an evangelistic youth concert?

The answer is simple. They have to use one of the following time-tested techniques:

The Soft Sell. "My church youth group is putting on this lame concert. I have to go, and I have to invite a friend. Would you please do me a favor and come with me?"

The Hard Sell. "Hey, you need to go with me to this church concert. If you don't, I won't be your friend anymore."

The Trade-Off. "Sure, I'll be glad to go with you to visit your grandma in the nursing home, but then you'll have to go to a church concert with me."

The Innocent Invitation. "I heard something about a concert at the amphitheater. I don't know much about it. It might even be some church thing. But, hey, we aren't doing anything on Saturday. Why don't we go check it out?"

The Alternative Activity. "My church youth group is sponsoring a concert at the amphitheater on Saturday. Let's go and sit in the back row. We can shoot spit wads at all the nerdy freshmen."

The Diversion (female style). "Hey, Erin. You know that cute guy, Scott, from my church youth group? He is going to be at a concert on Saturday. Let's go. I'll try to arrange it so you can sit next to him."

The Diversion (male style). "Hey, Drew. There's a concert on Saturday. There are going to be girls there."

Each technique can be tweaked to suit a teenager's personality and the circumstances. In no event, however, should a kid from the youth group resort to using the pastor's suggested form of invitation (known as the "evangelistic choice" technique): "Excuse me, [insert the name of your friend]. I'm taking a survey for my church youth group. Would you rather (a) go to a great concert on Friday night, or (b) spend eternity in hell?"

Brad, on the left, nonchalantly suggested to his friend, Keith, that they spend Saturday afternoon hanging out near the amphitheater in the park. Now Brad is trying to build up the courage to invite Keith into the concert. Unfortunately, Brad has waited too long. The concert is over and people are exiting from the amphitheater.

CHAPTER 36

How to Live a Double Life

The teenage years are bad enough, with all of the physical, mental, and emotional changes that kids go through, not to mention the constant pressure of being accepted by their peers. But then you add on the extra pressure of growing up in the church—with all of its unique traditions, customs, and beliefs—and the challenges are compounded. It isn't church that's the problem. Most kids who have been in and around church for most of their lives are very comfortable with the experience. It can be a safe haven, or "sanctuary," from all of their nonchurch activities. No, the challenge for church teenagers isn't going to church. It's the constant back-and-forth movement from their church experience and their life in the "world," which basically includes everything from Monday to Saturday.

In other words, the scenario is this: How do you move from the culture of the world to the culture of the church and back again—and repeat this every week—without slipping up once in a while and revealing your true identity? It's not easy, which is why this chapter on living a double life is so important. Just as the secret agents in the movies maintain separate identities for each of their worlds, church kids can live a perfectly normal double life as long as the following conditions are met:

(1) **They must dress differently for church than they do everywhere else.**

Notice the young man in the picture. He is wearing the quintessential church attire: white pants, white shoes, a plaid shirt, and a neat haircut. If this guy were to go to school looking like this, he would never make it home. The junior high or high school fashion police would beat him up verbally (and sometimes physically) so that he would never wear these  clothes to school again. However, wearing an outfit like this to church is not only acceptable, but also encouraged, especially if you are looking for a career as a gospel quartet singer. Wise double-life Christians maintain two wardrobes—one for church and one for every other occasion.

(2) **They must talk differently at church than they do everywhere else.**

This doesn't mean that the double-life Christian teenagers need to use bad language once they have stepped off the church campus. It's just that the church uses a language that is foreign to the outside world. Consider these basic church words and phrases:

Bought by the blood

Praise His name

Hallelujah!

Glory

Freewill offering

You will never hear teenagers use these words outside the church, where words such as "Hey, man," "totally," and "wasted" are the norm. The double-life Christian teen is adept at talking one way at church, and another way at home and at school.

(3) **They need to act differently at church than they do everywhere else.**

When double-life teenagers are at church, they are happy, enthusiastic, optimistic, and content. They also willingly talk to people who are twice their age, and they don't mind being nice to little kids. Outside the church, it's a different story. Double-life teenagers must appear unhappy, troubled, negative, and disgruntled. Adults are a pain and little kids get in the way. They must never be hopeful for the future and generally believe that nothing good can occur in this world.

There you have it. Three simple ways to live a double life and keep each life from interfering with the other. Of course, there is a downside. The pressure of living life as a secret agent Christian may prove to be too great. The only solution is to choose to live just one of the two lives. The question is, which one?

CHAPTER 37

How to Get a Teenager to Love Church

Many churches make the mistake of trying to lure teenagers to church with fantastic programs and activities. Time, energy, and resources of the church are devoted to operating the church coffeehouse (the *Solid Grounds Café*), the summer skydiving camp in Peru, and the Easter-week missionary trip to Maui. All these events are great. The kids love them. It gets the kids into the church, where they can hear about God.

That's actually the key to getting teenagers to love going to church. Not the activities, but learning about God. Sometimes, all of the programs and activities can obscure two fundamental principles of youth ministry:

God is cool. Very cool. We don't need to worry about changing His image to make Him relevant to teenagers. Our all-knowing, all-powerful, all-loving, eternal God wants to have a personal relationship with each teenager to guide him or her through life. You can't get more relevant than that.

Teenagers aren't dense. Contrary to the notion held by

some adults (and contrary to the image that some teenagers try to project), kids are perceptive. Very perceptive. They are smart enough to know a good thing when it is presented to them.

These two principles should guide every church's philosophy of youth ministry. Tell the kids about God, and they will be attracted to Him. It is as simple as that. Don't worry about getting the kids to love church. Introduce them to God, and they will fall in love with Him. (Learning to love church will be part of the natural progression of loving God.) God has everything that teenagers need. All the church needs to do is let the kids know who God is. Once the introduction is properly made, God can hold their attention.

May your roots go down deep into the
soil of God's marvelous love. And may you have
the power to understand. . .how wide, how long, how
high, and how deep his love really is. . . .
Then you will be filled with the fullness of life
and power that comes from God.

EPHESIANS 3:17–19

CHAPTER 38

How to Get Red Punch Stains Out of the Church Fellowship Hall Carpet

What is it about churches and red punch, specifically red *Hawaiian Punch*? Why is it the universal drink for all events in the church Fellowship Hall? Experts agree that churches are partial to red punch for the following reasons:

- It's zesty with no hint of worldly carbonation, so Baptists like it.

- Methodists are allowed to add 7-Up or Sprite for an even zestier taste.

- Presbyterians often add sherbet ice cream for real excitement.

- Red is a sacred color.

- Kids love it and adults don't mind.

- Red Hawaiian Punch comes in concentrated form for easy storage.

Whatever the reason, the average church keeps a five-year supply of red punch in the kitchen for all occasions. The only downside is that once you spill a cup on the carpet, it's almost impossible to extract. That's why every church Fellowship Hall in the country has a number of unsightly red punch stains in the carpet. For anyone interested in knowing how to deal with these spots, here are a few scenarios on how to remove them:

① **Make a gigantic batch of red punch and do a preemptive spill.**
The idea is to create one enormous red punch stain that covers the entire carpet so that the original carpet color is completely hidden. This way, any new spillage will simply blend into the giant spill that is now in the church carpet.

② **Install carpet that is already the color of red punch.**
This achieves the same effect as the first method, only you get to enjoy that new carpet smell until the first church social and someone inevitably spills red punch.

③ **Have a "healing" service for the carpet.**
Popular with Pentecostal churches, this method involves a special prayer meeting in which the church deacons "cast out" the stains, sometimes with the help of specially anointed carpet stain remover.

④ **Take out the carpet and install linoleum.**
Churches with less faith may want to try this scenario.

The only downside is that people will still spill red punch, thereby creating a slick surface, leaving the church unnecessarily exposed to possible litigation.

⑤ **Ban red punch altogether.**
This has been tried by many churches, but with mixed results. In some churches people begin to miss the cute red mustaches on all the kids' faces. Other churches try substituting the red punch with sparkling cider, causing even more controversy because of the wine-like appearance of the new drink.

If you have any other ideas or proven methods for red punch stain removal, please call the church red punch hotline at 1-800-RED-PUNCH. Operators are standing by.

Another way to get red punch stains out of the carpet is to make it a game.

CHAPTER 39

How to Make an Edible Covered-Dish Casserole

Few people will actually admit it, but there is cutthroat competition in the church. It occurs every time there is a church-sponsored potluck dinner. Each person or family is responsible for contributing to the meal. The instructions often go like this:

- Everyone should bring a covered-dish casserole.

- In addition, if your last name begins with A-M, bring a salad, or if your name begins with N-Z, bring a dessert.

- If you are not married, then bring a covered-dish casserole and rolls.

- If you are in the college/early career class, you can just bring rolls.

As you can see, this means that the only way you can escape bringing a covered-dish casserole to the church potluck is to be a member of the College/Early Career class. (This may be one of the reasons why there are a few single guys over the age of forty who are still hanging out in the college/early career class.)

A covered-dish casserole might seem mundane and

noncontroversial in the outside world, but it is the object of intense scrutiny and competition in the church-case scenario. There is often a not-so-secret society of certain church members who take sinful delight in determining who made the best casserole and who made the worst one. It is a type of Covered-Dish Casserole Sweepstakes. The unannounced winners are paid a reverence that is usually reserved for the apostles, while the easily identified losers suffer a disdain that is associated with Judas.

For most entrants, there is no desire to win. They just don't want to be the worst. In other words, if you are like most people, your casserole doesn't need to be gourmet; it just needs to be edible. Don't despair if you are a kitchen klutz. Here are three tricks you can use to achieve the mediocrity of an edible casserole contribution (or at least anonymity in the contest):

① **Buy your casserole at the deli.**
This is a violation of the unwritten rules, but nobody has to know. Simply take your own dish to the deli and fill it there. Don't make the rookie mistake of trying to transfer the contents from the deli's container into your dish while you are sitting in your car in the church parking lot. You risk leaving telltale spillage on your clothes. Also, the potluck police check the insides of the cars in the church parking lot during dinner.

② Don't put a name label on your dish.

It is the custom to write your name on a piece of masking tape that is affixed to the side of your dish. This rule is supposedly to facilitate the return of dishes to their respective owners after dinner. (But the real reason is to more easily identify the winners and the losers of the church's culinary contest.) If you resort to this trick, you'll have to abandon your dish at the end of the dinner. Retrieving a dish without a name label is an admission that you submitted a casserole that was so bad you didn't want your name associated with it.

In this photograph, the minister of music is caught switching the name labels on the casserole dishes.

③ **Use a pseudonym.**

You can't simply switch name labels on the dishes. Someone will request an inquiry by the church board if they see their name on your pot of beans and wieners. Instead of switching name labels, simply put a fake name on the masking tape on your dish. We suggest using an obscure name, such as Caroline Ferdinandsen. Of course, if people in the church know you, you'll have to be discreet when you deliver your dish to the church kitchen and when you retrieve it. (Or, you'll need to hire some stranger to go to the kitchen and say, "Hello, I'm Caroline Ferdinandsen. Where's my empty dish?")

If the whole church potluck scenario is intimidating to you, then skip it. Just go to the Olive Garden restaurant for a nice pasta dinner. You won't be missing an opportunity for fellowship with church members. You'll find many of them at the Olive Garden, along with everyone else who was intimidated by the casserole competition.

CHAPTER 40

How to Win a Church Softball Game

There aren't many church activities where competition is encouraged. This is mainly because spirituality is such a subjective thing. There's no measurement or score that shows one person or team defeating another in a game of "Best Christian" or "Gold Medal Sermon." There isn't any Spiritual Super Bowl or Heavenly World Series.

That's not to say that Christians aren't competitive. That same spirit that drives people to win in sports or business is still there in church, only it's buried beneath a thin spiritual veneer. That's why churches have softball teams. Years ago a very wise person decided that church members needed a safe, wholesome outlet for their competitive drive, and slow-pitch softball was chosen as the perfect game. There are several reasons for this:

- Unlike more aggressive sports like football and hockey, you don't need any special equipment or padding to play softball. It's a "whosoever will, may come" kind of sport.

- Girls and boys and men and women can play softball together, making it a sport for the whole "body."

- The very word "soft" in the name implies the spiritual virtues of gentleness and kindness.

- The object of the game is to score points by getting your teammates "home," which should be the goal of every Christian.

- When a team wins, there's no "in your face" celebration. Just an attitude of relief that the game is finally over.

Some highly organized churches participate in softball leagues with other churches. Less sophisticated churches manage to set up softball challenge matches at their annual church picnics. Should you ever find yourself a participant in a church picnic softball game, here are some tips on how

you can keep your competitive edge while maintaining good Christian sportsmanship. In other words, here's how to win a softball game in a spirit of love and grace.

① **It's perfectly acceptable to bring in "ringers" from outside your church.**
In the picture on the previous page you can see Gordie and Reuben, who play in a city softball league. Sometimes the promise of a great church picnic lunch is all it takes to convince guys like this to join the team. Of course, you must make an attempt to "witness" to them during the game.

② **It's a good idea to use "church chatter" when the other team is at bat.**
Regular chatter sounds like this: "Hey, batter batter, swing." Church chatter is more encouraging: "Hey, batter batter, you can do it." Under no circumstances should you ever say, "Hey, sinner sinner, you're going down."

③ **Certain gestures that are acceptable in regular sports are not suitable for church softball.**
These include—but are not limited to—

- chewing;

- spitting;
- scratching below the waist.

4 **There are certain gestures that are encouraged in church softball.**

These include—but are not limited to—

- the "windmill," indicating the Holy Spirit's anointing of your team;

- raising two hands, indicating thankfulness for the go-ahead run;

- praying on two knees, indicating that your team is losing badly and needs divine intervention.

CHAPTER 41

How to Enjoy a Couples' Retreat

Every year or two, someone from the church gets an urge to schedule a "couples' retreat." This person is always a woman. (Men get urges, but not for a couples' retreat.) The woman with the idea for a couples' retreat always finds support from the other married women in the church. Every married female thinks that a couples' retreat is exactly what is needed to whip their husbands into marital shape.

Despite the groundswell of female support for the couples' retreat, it won't happen automatically. The women of the church have a tough sales job ahead of them. The primary obstacle to scheduling a couples' retreat is the fact that the idea must meet with the approval of the men's ministry department. Usually, the leader of the men's ministry will be opposed to the couples' retreat proposal because he is a husband and doesn't want to be whipped into marital shape.

As far as couples' retreats are concerned, men and women have completely different perspectives:

A woman: She is anxious to attend a couples' retreat because it will give her the opportunity to have long discussions with her husband.

A man: He dreads the prospect of a couples' retreat because it will provide the opportunity to have long discussions with his wife.

It isn't that church men don't love and appreciate their wives. It is just that they prefer to cherish their wives in silence.

Given the fact that so many men are opposed to a couples' retreat, how come every church holds these retreats on a regular basis? The explanation is simple: Women are much smarter than men. Here is how it happens: Men make the mistake of appointing a married guy to be the leader of the men's ministries. The women are shrewd enough to appoint his wife as their representative for presenting the proposal for a couples' retreat to the church board. The leader of the men's ministries will invariably approve the proposal. Even though he may risk the anger of the other husbands in the church, this guy doesn't want to face the prospects of offending his wife. A ticked-off wife is far more dangerous than a mob of angry men.

So the couples' retreat is inevitable. No husband can escape it. It is just a matter of time. The committee that plans the retreat must anticipate that the husbands will be attending with attitudes that are less than enthusiastic. Special planning must be given to structure the retreat in such a manner that it is an enjoyable experience for both the men and the women. Here are a few suggestions to make the husbands feel more comfortable, which will make the wives happier:

① **Hold the retreat in separate facilities.**
The women can use a conference center and stay in rooms at the Ramada Inn. The men can rough it at Camp Runamuck.

② **Alternate the emphasis of seminar sessions.**
For every seminar on spousal communication techniques, there must be a corresponding session on some aspect of sports.

③ **Use food as a motivation for meeting attendance.**
Hold every seminar in the dining facility. Make sure there is a well-stocked, serve-yourself dessert buffet table.

④ **Avoid controversial terminology.**
Basically, this means that the guest speaker must eliminate any reference to the word "feelings."

We don't mean to suggest that every husband is a romantic doofus. It is just that they are like M&M's. To get to their soft and sweet center, you have to break through a tough outer shell. Keep this in mind if you want them to get sentimental. You might have to start by showing a video of the movie *Hoosiers*.

CHAPTER 42

How to Tell the Difference Between a Men's and Women's Conference

Nowhere are the differences between men and women so pronounced than at the conferences and retreats they attend. This comparison between these two types of events is not meant to be sexist in any way. This church-case scenario is merely intended to be a guide for both men and women so they will clearly know what the conferences of the opposite sex are really like, and in so knowing, gain a greater appreciation for their counterparts. So in the interest of promoting harmony, respect, and appreciation between the sexes, here is how you can tell the difference between a men's and women's conference or retreat.

① **The Setting**

Women enjoy a civilized and classy conference setting, such as a hotel or resort. There must be plenty of time in the daily schedule for women to change into different outfits, depending on weather and mood.

Since guys don't need to shower or shave when they are with other guys for a weekend, their accommodation needs are simple. They'll even put up with bunk beds and outdoor plumbing if the chow is hearty and hot. Guys at a retreat generally wear the same clothes all weekend.

② The Food

Not only is the setting of the conference or retreat important to women, but also the setting of the table. Whenever they are gathered around a table—whether it's to eat or to share (or both)—there must be a centerpiece to go with the "theme" of the conference. If there is food, the tablecloth, utensils, plates, and glasses must all coordinate.

All men care about is getting the food, preferably in an "all-you-can-eat buffet" style. They are perfectly comfortable sitting around a picnic table, on a rock, or even on the ground. They don't even need eating utensils, although they will take them if offered.

③ Icebreakers

Women's conferences and retreats are big on icebreakers in which they can ask and answer personal questions about their lives and the lives of their in-laws.

The only kind of "icebreaker" men like is a game

requiring them to do challenging things for points, and they will participate only if a winner is declared. In the men's retreat photo below, the men are getting to know each other by seeing who can most accurately imitate a baboon in heat.

④ The Speaker

Women like their conference speakers to be highly educated, high-achieving professional women who have broken out of the traditional roles imposed on them by men. Women also go for speakers who have a dynamic personal story of overcoming great odds.

Men prefer speakers who either currently coach or who in the past have coached a successful college or professional sports team. They don't mind hearing CEOs speak, as long as the speaker is the CEO of a sports management company. Men also go for speakers who have once been in prison but are now dynamic Christians.

(5) **Breakout Sessions**

Women's conferences and retreats typically feature seminars and "breakout" sessions so the attendees can get into smaller discussion groups for more intimate face-to-face conversation.

Men's conferences work best when all the guys are together in a big room, all facing the speaker. The only breakout sessions guys like are in a foursome playing golf on a nearby course during afternoon free time.

(6) **The Ultimate Conference**

The ultimate women's conference is held in a seven thousand-seat indoor arena, where they feel comfortable doing what women do in response to an especially good general session speaker: clap, nod, embrace the women next to them, and promise to make their husbands, boyfriends, or fathers into better men.

The ultimate men's conference is held in a fifty thousand-seat stadium, where they feel comfortable doing what men do in response to an especially good general session speaker: yell, scream, pump their fists, take off their shirts, high-five the guys around them, and promise to be better husbands, boyfriends, or fathers.

CHAPTER 43

How to Avoid the Church Fund-Raiser

Nobody likes the church fund-raiser (except the pastor and members of the church board). In fact, people try to avoid it. Consequently, references to the event are often disguised with terminology that sounds spiritual. Instead of being labeled as "The Money Drive," the fund-raising campaign is couched in religious jargon, such as:

"Together We Build"

"Gathering His Tithes and Offerings"

"Our Gifts to the King"

"He Gave Us His Son. What will You Give to Him?"

Any fund-raising campaign that is well orchestrated will include every church member getting a special envelope for his or her financial contribution. Each envelope is printed with the motto of the fund-raising campaign. The use of the envelope is always described in delicate terms. You are never told to "stuff your bucks in the envelope." Instead, you are told that the envelope is for your use in "fulfilling your faith pledge" or in "acknowledging your stewardship commitment."

If it is your intent to avoid any contribution to the church's fund-raiser, you are going to have to keep your wits about you. The spiritual pressure may be too strong to resist unless you take one of the following steps:

① **Change churches.**

This doesn't have to be a permanent move. It can be temporary. In communities where this ploy has been used extensively, the pastors have conspired to hold all their fund-raisers at the same time. If that is true in your community, then you've got no place to run.

This is Brittany's forty-seventh da of her self-impose. isolation at the church's recreation field. She will return to fellowship with the other church members at the conclusion of the fund-raising campaign.

② **Volunteer to work in the junior high department.**
If you offer this trade-off, most churches will be more than glad to exempt you from the fund-raiser. It is usually easier to get people to give money than to walk into a room of hyperactive, prepubescent junior high kids.

③ **Hide out in the nursery for the duration of the fund-raising campaign.**
We suggest hiding behind the "dirty diaper" bucket. No board member ever looks there.

If these techniques do not work, then you should plan to leave the country on a short-term mission trip. If you have your choice, you might as well select a place that has lots of beaches and a tropical climate. Hey, maybe the church fund-raiser can subsidize your trip.

CHAPTER 44

How to Let People Know Church Is a Good Thing

Churches often go to great lengths to reach new people. They sponsor rallies, revivals, and retreats to encourage prospective members to join. Churches produce creative advertising materials, such as flyers, newsletters, radio spots, and web sites, all designed and distributed so more people will know about what they have to offer.

There's nothing wrong with using promotion and advertising to tell others about your church, but there's a much more effective way to let people know that church is a good thing, and it doesn't cost a cent. And just what is this no-cost method of getting people interested in church? Why, it's you! *You* are the best way to encourage others to consider the value of church in their own lives.

Programs are nice, but church is more than a program. Buildings are nice, but church is more than a building. A powerful preacher is nice, but church is more than a powerful preacher. The church is *you*, someone who shares a common faith with hundreds of millions of people around the world.

It's great to be a member of your local church, and it's a life-changing experience when you become part of the universal church community of believers. But if we want to tell others about what we know, it's going to take more than being a member. We've got to show them by the way we live. Through His life and His words, Jesus showed us that love is the key—love for God, love for one another, and love for our neighbor. Love is what church is all about, and love is what we need to be about.

> *"So now I am giving you a new commandment: Love each other. Just as I have loved you, you should love each other. Your love for one another will prove to the world that you are my disciples."*
>
> JOHN 13:34–35

Afterword

Now that you have read our church-case scenarios, we want to hear yours. That's right! We are interested in receiving your stories and your photos of those church experiences that have made you into the person you are today (and we hope that's a good thing).

We're so serious about this that we've set up a special Web site for this purpose. All you have to do is log on at:

www.churchcasescenario.com

There you will find an interactive site filled with fresh stories and fun photos. And here's the best part: You will have the opportunity to submit your own church-case scenarios and pictures. We will regularly post the funniest, the most heartwarming, and the most creative submissions. Think of it as a kind of "Chicken Soup for the Church" with pictures.

So what are you waiting for? Start rummaging through your old photos and write down your fondest church memories. We can't wait to hear from you!

About the Authors

Bruce Bickel is an attorney, but he compensates for that
flaw by making a contribution to society as an inspira-
tional speaker for corporate and Christian events.
Bruce resides in Fresno, California, with his wife,
Cheryl. When he isn't doing lawyer stuff, Bruce is
active at Westmont College, where he has taught and
serves on the board of trustees.

Stan Jantz managed a chain of Christian retail stores for
more than twenty-five years. He is currently involved
in marketing and software development. Stan and his
wife, Karin, live in Fresno, where Stan is active in his
church and with Youth for Christ. Stan serves on the
board of trustees of Biola University.

Between them, **Bruce & Stan** have been
involved in church in one way or another for more
than eighty years. That includes attending church
services, choir practices, Bible studies, board meetings, summer camps and retreats, and Sunday school
classes. Through it all they have emerged as proud
proponents of the church.

Bruce & Stan have also found time to cowrite

forty books with more than two million copies sold, including the international best-seller, *God Is in the Small Stuff.* You can reach the guys through their web site: www.bruceandstan.com. Or you can e-mail them directly at: guide@bruceandstan.com.